Kitchen Witchcraft:
The Element of Water

Kitchen Witchcraft:
The Element of Water

Rachel Patterson

**MOON
BOOKS**

Winchester, UK
Washington, USA

JOHN HUNT PUBLISHING

First published by Moon Books, 2023
Moon Books is an imprint of John Hunt Publishing Ltd., No. 3 East Street, Alresford
Hampshire SO24 9EE, UK
office@jhpbooks.net
www.johnhuntpublishing.com
www.moon-books.net

For distributor details and how to order please visit the 'Ordering' section on our website.

ISBN: 978 1 78535 953 8
978 1 78535 954 5 (ebook)
Library of Congress Control Number: 2022948085

A CIP catalogue record for this book is available from the British Library.

Design: Lapiz Digital Services

UK: Printed and bound by CPI Group (UK) Ltd, Croydon, CR0 4YY
Printed in North America by CPI GPS partners

We operate a distinctive and ethical publishing philosophy in
all areas of our business, from our global network of authors to
production and worldwide distribution.

Contents

The sixth book in the Kitchen Witchcraft series along with *Spells & Charms, Garden Magic, Crystal Magic, The Element of Earth* and *The Element of Fire*.

This book will focus on the element of Water; what it is, the correspondences, how to work with it, elementals, meditations, rituals and basically everything water related.

Let's dive in...

Who am I?

I am a witch ... and have been for a very long time. I am also a working wife and mother who has also been lucky enough to write and have published a book or twenty-six. I love to learn, I love to study and have done so from books, online resources, schools and wonderful mentors over the years and continue to learn every day but have learnt the most from getting outside and doing it. I am High Priestess of the Kitchen Witch Coven and an Elder at the online Kitchen Witch School.

I like to laugh, bake and eat cake...

www.rachelpatterson.co.uk
facebook.com/rachelpattersonbooks

www.kitchenwitchhearth.net
facebook.com/kitchenwitchuk
Email: HQ@kitchenwitchhearth.net

www.youtube.com/user/Kitchenwitchuk
www.instagram.com/racheltansypatterson

My craft is a combination of old religion Witchcraft,
Kitchen Witchery, Hedge Witchery and folk magic.
My heart is that of a Kitchen Witch.

MY BOOKS

Kitchen Witchcraft Series
Spells & Charms
Garden Magic
Crystal Magic

The Element of Earth
The Element of Fire

Pagan Portals
Kitchen Witchcraft
Hoodoo Folk Magic
Moon Magic
Meditation
The Cailleach
Animal Magic
Sun Magic
Triple Goddess
Gods & Goddesses of England

Other Moon Books
The Art of Ritual
Beneath the Moon
Witchcraft ... into the Wilds
Grimoire of a Kitchen Witch
A Kitchen Witch's World of Magical Foods
A Kitchen Witch's World of Magical Plants & Herbs
Arc of the Goddess (co-written with Tracey Roberts)
Moon Books Gods & Goddesses Colouring Book (Patterson family)
Practically Pagan: An Alternative Guide to Cooking

Llewellyn
Curative Magic
A Witch for Every Season
Practical Candle Magic

Solarus
Flower Magic Oracle Deck

Water within me
Emotions around me
Intuition beyond me
Life fills me

The Basics

The elements are the original foundation of which all other things are made, by unification or transformation. The ancients divided the world into four basic elements which we know as Earth, Fire, Air, and Water. These four elements are vital to our survival, for without any one of them we could not exist. The four elements, five if you count ether/spirit, make up the base foundation of magic. We use them in ritual, energy work, healing and spell work.

We are all probably drawn more to one element than the others. They each have their own unique characteristics and properties that we can tap in to. They can be used individually or mix 'n' match to add power. I do think it helps to have a balance of them all.

In many myths and legends life first evolved from the primordial waters. We use the element of water every day to quench our thirst and to cleanse our bodies, a large proportion of our bodies are made up of this element that is governed by the moon.

Water is the element of the depths of emotion and of the subconscious. Water rules purification, the unknown, love and all other emotions. Water is associated with absorption and germination and pleasure, friendship, marriage, fertility, love, happiness, healing, sleep, dreaming, cleansing and psychic acts. Water rules physical things and places such as the womb, the unconscious mind, and any type of water source, from the largest oceans to the morning dew.

The place of water in the ritual circle is in the West, the place of death and transitions. The time of twilight and autumn are associated with water as these are mysterious times. You might find a cup or bowl of water on a witch's altar, but other representations may be a cauldron or shells. Our ancestors saw water as sacred and would give offerings at springs and other natural water sources, we carry on this tradition when we throw coins into fountains and make a wish.

If you live near the sea or a river then you might like to take a stroll along the water's edge, if the weather is good, you could even take a swim. If you aren't near natural water then take a long bath or go to the local swimming pool and if it rains go and stand outside in it, get soaking wet and relish every moment of it.

Here are a few of my own water correspondences:

Gender – Feminine

Animals – Beaver, cat, crab, crocodile/alligator, dolphin, dragonfly, duck, fish, flamingo, frog/toad, hippopotamus, lobster, newt, octopus, otter, pelican, penguin, seagull, seahorse, seal, shark, starfish, swan, turtle, walrus, whale

Colour – Blue, grey, green, white, black

Direction – West

Divination – Scrying, dowsing, pendulum

Energy – Receptive

Time – Dusk

Magic – Dream, mirror, divination, cleansing, protection, scrying, freezing, bathing, purifying

Symbols – water droplet, waves, triskele

Magical Tool – Chalice, cauldron, mirror

Musical Instrument – Cymbal, bell, singing bowl

Places – Lakes, springs, oceans, beeches, health spas, bathrooms, fountains, waterfalls, wells, rain

Spell work/Rituals/Positive Qualities – Purification, love, relationships, dreams, peace, compassion, emotions, nurturing, death, psychic abilities, sexuality, trust

Negative Qualities – Fear, jealousy, hatred, deceit, sorrow, spite, treachery
Season – Autumn
Spirits – Undines
Zodiac – *Pisces, Cancer and Scorpio*
Tarot – The suit of Cups
Pentagram position – Top left
Archangel – Gabriel

A bit obvious I know, but rivers, lakes and oceans are all made up from the element of water, which is a huge powerhouse of nature, never underestimate the power of the ocean. I love nothing more than retreating to the shores of the ocean to release any worries and issues and come home refreshed and renewed.

Rainwater can be collected in your garden in pots and buckets and water collected from wells is often classed as 'sacred' and water from the ocean is obviously already imbued with salt, so it packs an extra cleansing and purifying punch of energy.

If you don't have access to a river or the ocean then collect rainwater, use the tap in your kitchen or take a bath.

Asperging is a term often used in magic and basically it means sprinkling liquid (usually water or water with added herbs and oils) in order to achieve magical or spiritual cleansing. You can use water sprinkled on tools or herbs but also to cleanse an area ready for ritual or magical workings.

It is totally an intuition thing, but I work with water for:

Magical properties: Fear, flowing, purification, healing, soothing, love, emotions, cleansing, motion, psychic abilities, intuition, dreams, friendships, compassion, sadness, protection, trust, sympathy, rest and rebirth.

The Elemental You

Most of us will find that we are aligned more with one element than another. This may be affected by the zodiac sign we were born under; it may also be because of the work we do or the life we lead. Every mundane task carries a correspondence to one of the elements. The challenge is to create balance in ourselves between all four elements. You might like to make a list to see which element you are heavy in and which ones you might need to work a little more with to bring about balance. Let's look at the everyday element of water related tasks:

- Showering
- Bathing
- Swimming
- Washing the dishes
- Doing the laundry
- Crying
- Watering the plants
- Cleaning the bathroom
- Drinking (cold or hot in tea/coffee etc)
- Washing produce
- Washing the dog (or cat, or other pet!)
- Cooking/poaching/boiling/steaming
- Making/using ice cubes
- Flushing the toilet
- Brushing your teeth

Exercise

Make a list of all your daily chores and activities. Separate them into elements. Which element has the longest list? Which has the shortest? What could you do to help balance your elements out?

Water Energy

As we work with the positive and negative, sun and moon, masculine and feminine, energy too has opposites. Those of receptive and projective.

The flow of energy for the element of water is receptive. Receptive energy is also described as being feminine, soothing, passive, spiritual, calming, cold, attracting and magnetic. Receptive energy is good for absorbing negative energy and feelings, but also good for meditation, grounding and psychic abilities.

We can connect with water on a daily basis in very easy ways. The obvious being turning on a tap. There are also many magical ways to connect with the element of water too such as using your intuition. Along with all the mundane water element chores such as cleaning the toilet!

Just a reminder…when you work with energy, don't draw it from within yourself. That can be extremely draining and cause you to become very tired or even poorly. Use your body as a channel for the energy. Mother Earth is very happy to lend you the energy you need, all you must do is draw it from her and channel it to where you want it to go.

Water Magic

Several types of magic lend themselves to working with the water element.

Magical Water – water is readily available and wonderful to work magic with. You can turn it into magical or 'blessed' water very easily. The water can be used to anoint yourself, magical tools, spell pouches, candles or your altar. The water can be drunk to imbue the magic. Blessed water works well to cleanse and purify items or your home. Recipes for different types of magical water are included further in this book.

Freezing – Freezing magic is an excellent way to protect yourself or your family from negative energy or a person that is causing grief. This type of magic won't harm the person, just stop them from hurting you. Write the name of the person on a slip of paper and pop it in the freezer. To double up the protection you can drop the slip of paper with their name on into an ice cube tray, fill with water and then put it in the freezer.

Asperging – An asperger is a small brush used in ritual to sprinkle blessed water. It can be made from twigs, feathers or even something like lavender or rosemary stems tied together.

Saining – Sain is a Scottish word and means a method of ritual cleansing and blessing. You will need a bottle of water collected from a local source (spring, river or stream but rainwater will work as well). Preferably collected during the dark hours and on a waxing moon. Use the water to sprinkle in the corners of each room in your home or you can use it in ritual; stand together in a circle, each person takes a sip of the water then sprinkles water on the person to their left and passes the water on.

Ritual bathing – Preparation for any type or ritual or spell working often benefits from adding a ritual bath to your list. Add corresponding herbs and spices to your bath and take your time to visualise your upcoming ritual or spell whilst you bathe. Allow the water and herbs to release any negative energy you might be holding onto and bring in the positive. You can adapt this for a shower rather than a bath by charging your shower gel or soap with your intent. This also works by using visualisation with your daily ablutions. As you shower, wash or bathe, ask that the water remove any negative energy then bring in positive energy with your bathing products.

Washing away – Water releases, cleanses and purifies so it works well for clearing negative energy from your magical tools or crystals. Just place the item under running water or sprinkle with water. Be mindful some crystals are porous though! This also works well for disposing of spell remnants. These can be thrown into the ocean or rivers. BUT...please be mindful that anything thrown into water will have an effect on the eco balance of the water. Obviously never throw non-biodegradable items into water. I do sometimes throw herbs or flowers into the water, but it all has an effect, be mindful of this.

Negative energy, bad habits or emotions you wish to remove can be sent into a pebble or shell and then thrown into the ocean, river or pond to release. In the kitchen you can also release negative energy by visualising it being washed down the sink as you clean your vegetables.

Flushed away – Negative energy, bad habits or toxic relationships can be literally flushed down the toilet. Please don't flush spell remnants down the toilet! However, writing the name of a person you wish to remove from your life onto a sheet of toilet paper and flushing it away works very well. You can also write down bad habits or negative emotions you wish to release, jot them down on a sheet of toilet paper and flush it away, visualising it releasing as you do so.

Storm magic – Storms bring with them a huge powerful punch of energy so if there is a storm raging above you take advantage of all that magic. Torrential rain, thunder and lightning can be directed into all sorts of spell work. Work your spell with the storm overhead and visualise the energy from nature being directed down into whatever your magical working is. If you are feeling brave you can even stand outside in the storm and channel that energy through you, if you prefer to stay warm and dry then do your magical working by a window where you can see the storm. Obviously, it goes without saying that to stand on top of a hill in a lightning storm is not advisable.

Storm water cleansing:

Collect rainwater during a storm then add this to your bathwater and also rinse your hair in it. Ask for cleansing and renewal as you bathe. The same can be achieved by collecting rainwater during a storm then heating the water up in a cauldron and wafting the steam over your body.

Drinking – Any beverage can be charged with magic and then drunk to imbue the energy. The choice of beverage can also be tied in with your intent. Coffee brings an energy boost and clarity of a situation. Tea is good for meditation, courage, strength and prosperity. Water is good for releasing and emotions. And a glass of wine brings the magic of spirituality, happiness and love (one glass, not one bottle...). Beverages also make good offerings, pour a little onto the soil as a gesture of thanks.

Releasing – Whether it is in the form of throwing a pebble into the sea, flushing energy down the toilet or having a good ole cry, releasing is a necessary experience. We have a tendency to hold onto negative emotions, memories and energy. That all festers if we allow it to. Releasing let's go of that nasty festering energy and makes you feel all the better for it. Releasing also allows space for the good stuff to come in. Let it go...

Purifying/cleansing – Altars, sacred spaces, magical tools and crystals all benefit from regular purifying and cleansing. In fact, our own bodies need a regular spiritual cleanse on occasion too.

Purifying and cleansing clears out any negative vibes that have attached themselves, creating a blank canvas for us to charge with a fresh intent. Magical tools and particularly crystals also hold onto the energy of the last spell working, it will behove you to clear it out before starting a new spell. Otherwise energies can get very confused and spell working can go haywire. There are many methods of cleansing and purifying but water works particularly well. You can run an item under the tap or sprinkle it with blessed, moon or salt water.

Floor wash – Not just for your floors, a spiritual wash can be used for surfaces and windows too. Add a few herbs tied in a muslin bag, or a few drops of essential oil to a bucket of warm water and you have created a magical floor wash. Herbal tea bags work incredibly well for this. I like to add peppermint to my floor wash as it brings the magic of cleansing, protection and healing. Experiment with different herbs and see which works best for you.

Spritzers – These are so easy to make and create such a wonderful magical space.

You will need:

A Spritzer/misting bottle
90ml/3 fl oz distilled (boiled, then cooled) water
12 drops essential oil (your choice)

Pop the water and the oils into the bottle and give it a little shake. Spritz your face or body when you have a hot flush or need brightening up. The oils can also be used in a diffuser to cool and calm the energy in a room down or create a sacred space. This works well if you cannot use smoke to cleanse a room.

Time

Another association for the elements is the time of day. Water links to dusk, that evening twilight time of the day as the sun is setting until it becomes night-time. Dusk is one of those in-between times when magic is powerful. If you want to add a watery boost of energy to your spell working, then time your magic to happen at dusk.

Exercise

Work spells at different times and record the results, does it make a difference?

Symbols

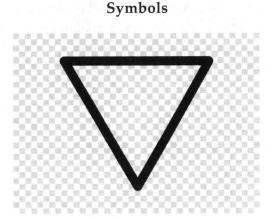

Probably the most recognised symbols for the elements are the triangles. Water is represented by a downward facing triangle. The downward triangle represents feminine energy and the Goddess. It also resembles the shape of a chalice and symbolises the womb.

If you want to represent water on your altar, in ritual or for spell work there are several items you can use.

A bowl of water – perhaps an obvious one, simple but effective.

A shell – perfect as it represents the ocean.

A pebble – from the ocean or riverbed brings in the elements of water and earth.

Triskele – symbol or triple spiral is an incredibly old image. The name comes from Greek, meaning 'three legs'. The spirals are thought to represent different things such as birth, death and rebirth and the mental, physical and spiritual self. It is also thought to represent the land, sea and sky. It is the latter meaning that aligns it with the element of water.

A spiral – symbol for me represents the Crone goddess and the journey of life, it can also show the flow of water.

The Vesica Pisces – comprises two spheres which intersect. The name is Latin and translates as 'bladder or vessel of a fish'. Some believe it to be a symbol of Jesus Christ and the image is also said to be found in the Ark of the Covenant. We use it in Paganism to represent the joining of the God and the Goddess or the Divine Feminine. In sacred geometry it forms the basic pattern for the Flower of Life and the Tree of Life. It symbolises harmony, strength and power.

The Awen – the word Awen is Celtic and means inspiration or essence. It is formed from three rays leading up to three dots and surrounded by a circle. The Awen symbol is used to represent modern day Druidry. Each ray has a different meaning such as mind, body and spirit or land, sea and sky, or nature, knowledge and truth.

A cauldron – representative of the feminine and water, also very useful!

A chalice – representative of the feminine and water.

The Chalice/Cup

Often used in ritual to share and pass around the ceremonial wine, or in the case of our coven in the winter, hot chocolate. In some rituals the words 'may you never thirst' are said after sipping from the communal chalice. The chalice is basically a cup. A chalice is also used to hold the sacred or blessed water for ritual. The chalice represents the feminine and the womb of the Goddess which aligns with the element of water. In Wiccan ritual the chalice is often used with the athame to represent the union of female and male energy. You will find the use of a chalice in many religious practices. Ceremonial chalices are often ornate designs of silver or pewter. But they can be made from any material, I have seen some beautiful turned wooden chalices. You don't need to use a fancy chalice, a glass or tumbler will work just as well. Take a look in charity/thrift stores as they are good places to find odd decorative glasses or cups that could be used. A metal or ceramic chalice can also be used in place of a cauldron to hold a charcoal disc and incense. It can also be utilised for scrying, fill with water and take a look. Use it to mix essential oil blends or tinctures as well. Fill a chalice with water and float a tealight candle on top. Pop your crystals into a chalice and leave under the moonlight to cleanse and charge them. You can use your chalice in a lot of similar ways to your cauldron.

The Cauldron

There can't be a more iconic symbol for a witch than a cauldron. In fact, the cauldron is a very practical and useful magical tool. Probably my own personal favourite and most used magical item.

Collins Dictionary definition: *A cauldron is a very large, round metal pot used for cooking over a fire. In stories and fairy tales, a cauldron is used by witches for their spells.*

A cauldron shaped pot has been used for centuries for cooking and boiling, usually hung over an open fire. The shape of the cauldron hasn't really changed at all. The cauldron is often used in ritual today to represent the feminine and the womb of the Goddess, much as the chalice is.

The cauldron does have many uses other than cooking and boiling water. I tend to use mine primarily for holding small fire ceremonies, to safely contain a candle and to contain a charcoal disc to burn incense. The cauldron works extremely well for this because they are usually cast iron and thus fireproof. The cauldron can also contain water for cleansing or consecrating. It can work well for all kinds of divination, fill with water for scrying, reading flames or smoke or wax readings. Use the cauldron as a portal, a gateway into other worlds, this works particularly well if you fill the cauldron with water. The cauldron also works well to hold offerings. If you are short of space, a cauldron can also be used as a portable, self-contained altar.

The *Tale of Taliesin* from the Welsh Mabinogion tells us of the goddess, Cerridwen, using a cauldron to brew the Awen, the source of inspiration. The cauldron is also a symbol of rebirth and renewal, linking to its shape as a womb, giving birth to new life. In Russian and Slavic folklore, Baba Yaga flies through the air in a large cauldron. You will find numerous other stories throughout folklore and myths that mention cauldrons. They aren't always associated with goddesses, there are tales of gods using cauldrons too. One example is the Celtic god, Dagda and the Undry, the Cauldron of Plenty, one of the four treasures of the Tuatha de Danann. Many of the stories tell of the cauldron providing abundance or rebirth in some way.

And of course, the cauldron can be used for cooking and brewing up potions. Whilst the cast iron cauldron is traditional and practical, albeit quite heavy to lug around, you don't have to spend lots of money on one. Look around in the charity/thrift stores for old casserole dishes or a crock pot, metal or ceramic ones can be found quite often.

Invoking and Banishing Pentagrams

You can use a pentagram to invoke or banish the elements in ritual. Each element starts and ends with a different point of the pentagram. The symbols are drawn in the air using your finger, a wand or an athame. As you draw the image, visualise it appearing in the air before you.

To call the element of water start with your finger, wand or athame at the top left-hand point of the pentagram and draw a line across to the right, then down to the left and continue around the pentagram.

To banish the element of water, perform the action in reverse, starting from the top right-hand point of the pentagram and drawing a line across horizontally to the left and then down to the right, following the rest of the pentagram.

To Dare

In modern Wicca, the Witch's Pyramid features the four elements plus that of spirit. It is not actually a physical pyramid but forms the shape of one. Each point represents one of the elements and this can be reflected in the pentagram shape too. Water represents 'to dare'. Bring out your roar! To dare is about being courageous and believing in yourself and your own abilities. Trust your intuition and have faith that you are on the right pathway.

Instrument

The bell, a cymbal or singing bowl are all associated with the element of water. Any of these can be used in ritual or spell work. They are particularly useful for clearing away negative energy and healing work. A bell or small cymbals are usually easy to obtain. Personally, I believe that singing bowls need to be researched before purchasing. Each singing bowl has a different tone, and you will need to find the one that resonates with you.

The Elementals

The Elementals are the energies of nature itself; they are the forces of the elements. They are true energy and have the characteristics of the element they belong to. They can take on any shape, size or form to deal with a particular task.

Elementals can charge us with energy; they can work with us on a physical, mental, emotional and spiritual level. Learning to work with them can tune us in to connect with the energy of nature around us. The Elementals interweave their energy patterns to create and keep all of nature, all of life on our planet.

Elementals have nothing to obstruct them, they can move through matter with ease, but they also need to connect with us to help with their own spiritual growth and evolution. In ancient Greece they were referred to as the kings of the four winds. Ancient Egyptians saw them as four sons of Horus. And the Norse had four dwarves, each one holding up a corner of the world.

In modern Wicca each group of Elementals has a higher being that looks over them, a King. Overseeing the Kings are Archangels. It is quite a hierarchical set up. There are, as you know four elements, so there are four Elementals, four Elemental Kings and four Archangels.

Archangel Gabriel

I am pretty sure I played the part of the Archangel Gabriel in a school nativity play once, I remember the coat hanger and tinsel halo...

The Archangel Gabriel has a direct communications line to us humans. If anyone is going to bring a message, then he is the delivery boy. Gabriel was the messenger that delivered the news to Daniel a messiah was on the way. His name translates as 'The strength of God'. He also has connections to the Moon and thus the element of water. In that role he helps with our imagination, intuition and our unconscious thoughts. I use the term 'he' but actually Gabriel has been seen as both male and female.

King Niksa/Nixsa

Quiet and unassuming he brings an air of calm and tranquillity. He is totally relaxed and at ease and can pass that energy onto others. He does speak with emotion and sincerity but in a totally laid-back manner. This guy puts you totally at ease, you would end up telling him your life story in a second. And those are exactly the qualities that he deals with, emotions, relaxation, calming energy and putting you at ease. This is one chilled out hippy dude.

Undines

An Undine is a water sprite of sorts, more primal than a mermaid (or merman) but more developed than a basic water sprite – somewhere in between! These Elementals are the force of Water. It can be springs, rivers, oceans, lakes, wherever there is a source of natural water. Water is life, we can't survive without it. The Water Elementals can help us find our inner source, they can help us to find and work with our empathy, healing and purification.

Undines work to keep our astral bodies in shape, to help us feel the connection to nature. They help us to open up to our psychic abilities, our emotions, creativity, intuition and our imagination. To live life to the full and experience all that is available to us. If you dream of water, the sea or rivers that could be the Undines at work. Ask for their help in dream work, they can aid you in lucid dreaming and astral travel.

Not connecting with the Undines regularly can cause us to become unbalanced and we could find our bodies clogging up with toxins. But again, be careful as too much work with the

Undines can cause us to become overly emotional. On a physical level it can also manifest as water retention. You may become self-absorbed, and your imagination might run away with you, making you overly sensitive and fearful.

Water Elemental Shapeshifting Meditation

Close your eyes and take a few deep breaths. Feel yourself becoming calm and relaxed with each out breath, letting go of all the worries of the day.

Feel any tension leave your body as we prepare to shape shift with the elements.

Now turn to face the West and the direction of the element of water. Visualise, feel and sense this element in whatever form is appropriate for you. This could be a gentle flowing river, the crashing of the ocean waves, a luxurious bubble bath or perhaps a clear puddle. Focus on your image and breathe it in, deep down into your abdomen and into your being. Let the element of water fill your entire body until you feel yourself dissolve and become one with the water. Stay with this element for a couple of breaths ... gradually let the water recede from your body until it is only in your belly, then release it completely with your next out breath. Take a few deeper breaths now and when you are ready open your eyes.

Welcome back to your human form.

Exercise

Work with the elemental meditation and keep a record of your experiences.

Working with Water

Water Magic

Although water in general has the same magical properties no matter what source it comes from, you can be more specific with the uses if you prefer, here are some suggestions for magical properties depending on the body of water:

Dew – Beauty, health and sight.

Fog – Balance, creativity, partnerships and hidden secrets.

Rivers – Cleansing, protection, direction and moving forward.

Streams – Cleansing, purification, harmony and dispelling.

Lakes/ponds – Reflection, relaxation, peace, calm, contentment and inner work.

Rain – Cleansing, protection and energy.

Ocean – Manifesting, power, health, energy and purification.

Springs – Blessings, cleansing, protection, growth and abundance.

Swamps/marshes – Binding, banishing and hexing.

Wells – Wishes, healing, intuition and inspiration.

Waterfalls – Energy, power, prosperity and success.

Snow & ice – Transformation, creativity, balance and peace.

You can work all sorts of spells using fresh water or salt water to bring the power of lakes, rivers and oceans to your magic. Collect fresh river or stream water if you can, otherwise bottled water works well and if all else fails use tap water. If you want to 'clean up' the tap water and get rid of some of the impurities and chemicals, you can boil the water first. If you have been lucky enough to collect fresh sea water that works extremely well but you can make your own salt water by adding...salt to water (yep you got it).

Rivers and oceans are perfect for 'washing away' feelings, bad habits and spell leftovers. Tipping old herbs left over from spell work into running water washes them away. You can write petitions on slips of paper and cast them into the ocean or rivers to allow the energy of water to work its magic.

If you don't have access to a natural source of running water, you can substitute the tap in your kitchen to wash away spell work. If you need to get rid of something, then flushing it down the toilet works perfectly (but please make sure it is biodegradable).

Rivers, Lakes, Ponds and More

Rivers, lakes, ponds, seas, oceans and any other names for large bodies of water and all with immense magical powers. Water is a necessity of life, never underestimate its power.

Rivers and streams have the ability to 'flow'. They bring movement so they are brilliant for removing or getting rid of things whether it is spell work that focuses on removing or dispelling or whether you just want the water to carry your spell away to 'do its thing' but please remember not to drop anything into any water system that won't safely degrade – not plastics or chemicals please.

The oceans and seas work well because of the power they have and the fact that they have built in cleansing and purifying properties because they are salt water. Ponds and lakes are slightly different because they don't tend to move much, they don't usually have waves and they don't flow like rivers, but they still hold the natural magic of water.

Wells

Water for drinking and washing has been drawn up from below the ground by the use of wells for centuries. In the UK the dressing of wells dates back to the mid-1300s, although it is believed the tradition dates back even further to the ancient Celts honouring the spirits of the water. Villages in England seemed to pick up the tradition again during the plague, making offerings to the wells and dressing them with flowers to honour the water and protect them from disease. The practice of well dressing waned over time but it has since had a revival thanks to the Victorians and a number of English villages continue the tradition. Wells are dressed with flowers, often in the form of images and scenes where the flowers, leaves and petals are stuck to wooden boards with the aid of clay to create a picture. Ancient Romans had a history of honouring wells and fresh springs often by leaving offerings or throwing coins into the water. Occasionally you might find an old well in a village, but they aren't seen so often nowadays. If you have one locally to you then it is an excellent place to leave an offering. Although, as always, please make sure it is biodegradable. Also be mindful if you do throw things into the water, some metals can leech out and even plant matter can contaminate the water source. Perhaps stick with the old idea of well dressing.

Exercise

Create your own well, not an actual hole in the ground but something symbolic. Use a glass or jar and fill it with water, then charge the water under the sun or moon. Then decorate the edge of the cup or around the base using flowers, herbs and crystals. Use the 'well' to make offerings and cast wishes. Or you could create your own well dressing image using a board, some clay and natural materials.

Sea Cleansing

If you feel the need to really cleanse and purify and rid yourself of negative energy, then you can petition the spirit of the sea to help you out. You can address the pure spirit of the ocean or pick a water deity to assist you. Visit the seashore and take six roses with you. Stand with your feet just in the water and one by one dip each rose into the seawater and then run it from your head down your body, your arms and your legs stroking downwards then throw each rose into the sea. Once you have done this with all six roses walk deeper into the water (up to your waist works well but if you don't feel comfortable go in as far as you can). Allow the waves to flow around your body six times asking for cleansing and renewal as you do so. Then turn and walk out of the water.

Consecrating

To consecrate, purify or charge an amulet with water energy. Fill a bowl with water, either fresh or salt depending on whether you want the power of fresh water or sea water. Hold your chosen amulet or tool above the bowl and visualise the ocean or a river (whichever you choose) swirling around the item. If the amulet or tool are water safe (i.e., they won't be damaged) then dip it into the water and say your intent out loud or even, make up a chant.

Making Magical Water

Blessed, charged or magical water – whatever you want to call it is super simple to make. Blessed water can be used for all sorts of things such as anointing (yourself, candles or magical tools), for consecrating and cleansing tools, adding to spell workings, ritual baths or even to drink.

Moon Water

You start with water (unsurprisingly), and it is your choice whether you use filtered, spring, tap water or collected rainwater. If you are worried about using tap water and all the icky stuff that is supposed to be in it, you can boil it first and allow it to cool. Then you need to put it in a container, and I find that a glass jar works very well. At this point if you feel the urge, you could charge and cleanse the water by holding your hand over the top and sending your intent into the water or you could waft some sage or incense over the top.

Then you need to place the jar in the light of the moon, you can put it outside, but I would put a lid on the jar. However, you can also sit it indoors on a windowsill it just needs to be able to catch the light of the moon. The full moon works well for this, but you could put water out in each phase of the moon and then you have different types for different spell workings.

Sun Water
Sun water can be made the same way but obviously, you put it in sunlight instead. You can stand it out in the sunlight to capture the individual phases of the sun; sunrise, morning (waxing), midday (full), afternoon (waning) and sunset.

Storm Water
Storm water is an interesting one to make as well, pop your jar of water outside or on the windowsill when there is a storm raging, it collects some powerful energy that you can then use when you need it.

Rain Water
Cleansing, refreshing and full of life-giving energy, rainwater replenishes and nourishes and can be used for those magical purposes.

Snow Water
Snow water can be made and all you need to do is scoop up some clean snow (I don't need to remind you not to use yellow snow, do I?) and pop it in a jar and allow to melt.

Ghost Water

Ghost water can be made by putting a bottle of water on a grave overnight during a full moon, remove before dawn. This can be used for hexing.

Rainbow Water

If you can catch some of the rain that falls whilst the rainbow is visible, then this can be used as blessed water in magical workings to bring the power of the rainbow.

Brackish Water

Brackish water is defined by its salt content. It is not fresh water, but neither is it seawater, it lies somewhere between. Brackish water is often created in an estuary where the river meets the sea. It brings about the magical quality of combining and merging together along with balance. Brackish water is not suitable for drinking, but it works well for magical use.

Lake Water

Lakes are generally still and calming with reflective surfaces, water collected from here will have those magical properties.

River Water

Rivers flow, sometimes slowly meandering along other times rushing quickly. River water represents time, patience and movement.

Sea Water

The power of the ocean is reflected in the magical properties that sea water brings. It is dark and light, cleansing and destructive. I think the ocean is often underestimated in terms of the power over life and death that it commands. Sea water can be collected and used for magical purpose, please don't drink it.

Spring Water

Spring water is natural and fresh and good to drink. Often spring water can be found at sacred spots (such as Glastonbury or Bath). It carries a very special kind of magic and the energy of the place. If you don't have a natural spring nearby take a look in the shops for bottled spring water, they will always state the location of the water source.

Flower Water

You can make magical water by infusing it with the power of flower blossoms it then takes on the magical properties of the flower that you used. It is easy to make but I would recommend using wildflowers or ones grown in your garden because you don't know what process bought flowers have been through.

One method is to collect your flower petals and pop them in a jar, cover with boiling water and allow it to sit for a day (or overnight) then strain. Use straight away, the remainder can be kept in the fridge for a short time. Another method is to use fresh flower petals and pour over just enough water to cover them. Simmer gently in a pan until the petals become limp. Strain and allow to cool. Use within a day or two, keeping the liquid in the fridge.

Crystal Water

Water (or any liquid come to that, although water is generally pure and takes on the energy of the crystal well) can be charged with the magical power of a crystal. You can even get special water bottles that have crystal infills. But crystal water or crystal elixir as it is often called, is easy to make yourself. You will need to check that the crystal is SAFE to drop into water, make sure it won't disintegrate and that it isn't toxic, as that would be bad...very bad.

Crystal essence is water that has been imbued with the energy of a single specific crystal. An elixir is usually a mixture of essences blended with an intent in mind. The most straightforward way to create a crystal essence is to drop a crystal into a glass or bottle of water. Cover with a lid and leave in the sunlight or moonlight for a while, a few hours or overnight will be fine.

The safer method is to put the crystal inside a container before popping that into water. This way you make sure that no toxic elements leak out directly into the water. Place the crystal in a small glass or bottle and then place that into a larger container that has the water in.

Your prepared crystal essence can then be mixed with another made from a different crystal to combine the energy or used on its own. The water can be drunk, add to the power by stating your intent before you sip the water. Use to bathe an area of your body or add to bath water. Anoint your pulse points, chakras, altars or magical tools. Dab onto candles and pouches for spell work. Feed your plants with the water. Sprinkle around your home to clear out negative energy.

Dream Magic

I think dream magic aligns with the energy of water. It is all about emotions and intuition. Working with your dreams and understanding their meanings can be fascinating, as can lucid dreaming and astral travel, although the latter two can be quite difficult to master.

Dreams are messages sent by your mind, from your subconscious and I think the best person to interpret the meanings of your dreams is you. There are lots of books out there that will give you the basic meanings of symbols seen in your dreams but ultimately it is your dream, your conscious and therefore you are the best qualified to interpret the meaning. A dream is made up of your thoughts, your concerns, your worries, your hopes, your wishes, your desires, your memories and maybe even events that have yet to happen. Why are dreams often so muddled and confusing? Well the mind is a complicated thing, it has a lot of information stored and when we dream it tries to send all the information at once, it is then up to us to filter through it. Everyone dreams, you might not always remember them, but we all do. Dreams can be a source of insight into ourselves, they can also help us cope with situations where we need a bit of guidance. Or they can just simply make us feel good (or bad depending on the type of dream).

How can you remember your dreams? Yep, I know the feeling, you have had an amazing dream but once you get out of bed it has gone and no matter how hard you try to grab hold of those thoughts and images they are gone. So, there are a few hints and tips:

- Just before you go to sleep charge a glass of water with your intent to recall your dream fully and completely on waking, drink the water and then lay down to sleep.
- Place a crystal under your pillow that has the specific energies and qualities to help you recall your dreams.
- As soon as you wake, don't move, lie still. Take a deep breath and recall the entire dream, replay it back in your mind, really 'feel' all the details, the images, the senses and the scents. Replaying it once you have woken but not actually got up yet helps to set the images into your conscious mind.
- Keep a notebook beside your bed and when you wake, make sure you don't even sit up in bed, just grab the pad and jot down some notes, it doesn't have to be the whole novel just some key points to jog your memory once you are fully awake. You don't necessarily have to recall the entire dream, just the key snap shots that seem important will be enough.

- It is often quite interesting to keep a specific dream journal, note down your dreams from each night, you can then refer back to them at a later date and hopefully glean a lot more information and insight from them.
- When you recall your dream ask some questions:

What topic was my dream set on?

What energy did it involve?

What was the most important part of the dream?

What message is it trying to convey to me?

How can I work with the information brought to me?

What parts of the dream are based in reality?

What parts of the dream really influence me?

Who was in the dream and who did they represent?

What did my senses feel? Heat/light/dark/cold etc

What voices did I hear?

What colours were in my dream?

Do I have any reoccurring themes or symbols in my dreams?

Lucid Dreaming – When we become aware of what we are dreaming and when we are able to interact with our dreams – that is lucid dreaming. Once you are able to find your dream energy centre and how to work with it the more successful you will become at lucid dreaming. Lucid dreaming is all about being in control of your dream not in a 'control freak' kind of way but in a way that you try to understand your dream and use the energy to help.

I think lucid dreaming is a step on from daydreaming or meditation dreaming. You can go into a lucid dream with a question or a query, approach it with an open mind and with the idea that the dream will be productive.

An important aspect of lucid dreaming is to have the ability to become aware when you are in the dream, that awareness then becomes your point of lucidity. You will need to study your own sleep patterns to work out the best time for you, when you can work with dream lucidity best. You will need to think about 'reality checks' this will show you whether you are actually lucid dreaming or not. It might be something simple like touching the earth with your fingers, you know what that feels like in the real world, so it is a good check in the dream world – if it feels right then you are lucid dreaming. Do something that you can recognise the feel of. Practice these reality checks in your mind first before you enter the dream state. Actually, staying in lucid dream mode does take some work, it is all about keeping that fine balance between being in the dream state but being lucid enough to explore further. Stay calm and relaxed, follow where you believe it is taking you, if you hit resistance take your dream in another direction.

Astral Travel – Sometimes called astral journeying, astral projection or an out of body experience. It means that the part of you, your true inner self leaves your physical body and travels to another reality or another place. Every living thing has an etheric counterpart. The lower etheric plane is quite a dangerous place, if you find yourself there during and out of body experience it is recommended to quickly raise your vibrations and change your trip by looking upwards to find a better level, it may be signified by a bright white light or lots of bright colours. The higher etheric plane, sometimes called the high astral or spiritual plane, is a very spiritual place, this is where you will find incredibly wonderful spiritual beings.

I believe that there are many, many etheric planes in between the higher and the lower planes.

The astral plane itself is a very emotional place, we are after all sending our astral self there which is full of emotions. Hopefully your astral experiences will be wonderful and interesting but please beware that sometimes they can be a bit scary and occasionally unpleasant. It is our own level of vibrations that determine which level of plane we visit. Remember, you are always in control.

So why would you want to astral travel? Well it is a good way of visiting those that have passed on, it is also a way of travelling to interesting places, to learn, to experience, to gain knowledge and insight. And of course, the astral plane isn't restricted by time or dimension!

As I mentioned before, astral travel can be difficult, it can take some time to master. It does take practice. We can leave our physical body once we are in a very relaxed state, that moment just between sleeping and waking.

There are various methods for performing astral travel, here are some ideas:

Determine a location that you want to visit on the astral plane. Sit in a comfortable position, somewhere quiet where you will not be disturbed. Focus on your breathing.

Method 1:
When you are in a calm, centred and relaxed state, try to separate your astral body from your physical body, starting by visualising it floating a foot or so above your physical body. Then you can send your astral body to wherever you want to, visualise your destination and send your body there.

Method 2:
Another method is to expand your body roughly half an inch with each breath. This is done only with visualisation, is fairly easy to do, and often produces fast results. When you have expanded to roughly twice your normal size,

continue the process with even greater dimensions. Inches become feet, and feet become miles, and so on. Don't worry too much about the actual act of leaving your body. One variation of this technique consists of proceeding little by little. For example, the first few times you would only move your astral arms out of your physical body, a bit later your whole upper body and head, and so on. Always keep in mind that obtaining the remote information is your actual goal, regardless of how you get there, and not necessarily the act of buzzing around in an astral body.

Method 3:

Start with the basics, using either of the methods above to separate your astral body, but instead of disappearing off to the Bahamas; take an astral walk around your home. Feel your astral body strolling around the rooms in your house and remotely viewing all that they contain.

Method 4: The Fixed Anchor

After reaching the trance state, focus on a point outside of the physical body (e.g., at the end of the bed). You can either simply focus on a point in space, or you can imagine an object at that point (it usually helps if it is a familiar object). Once you can clearly see the focus point in your mind's eye, 'feel' how solid it is. Try pushing it around with your mind, try pulling it, or moving it. The focus point should be totally solid and entirely 'fixed' where it is. No amount of mental manipulation should be able to move it.

Once the focus point is totally fixed, imagine reaching out with your arms and grabbing hold of the focus point (object). Remember, this WILL NOT MOVE. Now, try pulling the object towards you, gently at first, and then harder and harder.

Gradually as you pull you will feel yourself moving towards the focus point (instead of vice versa). Finally, you will find yourself at the focus point outside your physical body – Presto, you've done it.

Returning

Once you want to return your astral body to your physical one, ask for permission first, and then slowly re-connect. Take your time doing this you don't want to leave anything unconnected.

Places

There are certain places and locations that align with the element of water. If you can take yourself off to visit them to connect. If that isn't possible crack out your visualisation skills and meditate to take yourself there.

Roman Baths

Found in the centre of the beautiful city of Bath, Somerset, are the Roman Baths. Home to the goddess Sulis, it is an incredible experience to visit. Built around a natural hot spring, that it seems was a place of worship long before the Romans arrived, it is a very magical place. If you get the chance to visit, I highly recommend it, if you are unable to, then meditation is an option.

Find a quiet place where you won't be disturbed and make yourself comfortable. Take a few deep breaths in and out.

As your world around you dissipates you find yourself standing in a courtyard, large stone slabs beneath your feet. In front of you is a set of plate stone steps and as your eye leads you upwards you see at the top each side is flanked by columns, supporting a stone fascia.

In the centre is what looks like the face of a man, carved into the stone, with wild hair fanning outwards from his face and a snake torc around his neck.

You move forward towards the stone steps and take the first step up, and then the next, upwards towards the entrance. Step 3, 4, 5, 6, 7 and 8.

At the top of the steps you see an open doorway, so you walk through.

Inside it is warm and you feel a slight moisture in the air.

The floor is a beautiful mosaic pattern that leads you down a corridor, so you follow.

At the end of the corridor you turn right which leads you out into the open air.

In front of you now is a large rectangular pool of water, clear and inviting.

There are other folk in the water, bathing and some sitting around the pool side.

You feel a presence and turn to see an attendant offering you a robe and gesturing for you to step to the side and undress.

You follow their lead, and they take your clothes from you, folding them neatly and handing you the robe.

You step back to the edge of the pool, disrobe and step down into the water. You are surprised to find it is pleasantly warm.

You sink into the waters but find you can easily touch the floor with your feet.

Drifting, you allow the warm water to soothe and heal you.

The waters release and let go any fears or worries, taking them away from you.

Spend some time here…

When you are ready, make your way back to the steps and slowly come up out of the water.

As you do so, the attendant holds out your robe for you.
You feel lighter, more relaxed and completely refreshed.
You step out of the robe and back into your clothes.
Make your way back now, down the corridor with the mosaic floor and out of the entrance.
Take each step down, one at a time. 1, 2, 3, 4,5 6, 7 and 8 until you are in the courtyard.
Turn and look back at the face in the stone above the entrance.
Then slowly and gently come back to the here and now.

Open your eyes and wriggle your fingers and toes.

Chalice Well

At the top of a hill that leads down into the town of Glastonbury, Somerset, you will find the Chalice Well. Contained within pretty gardens is a natural spring and a well. It is a quiet and tranquil place. If you cannot get there to visit, then try this meditation.

Find a quiet place where you won't be disturbed and make yourself comfortable. Take a few deep breaths in and out.

As the world around you dissipates you find yourself standing outside a small wooden gate. The sun is shining, and you can hear the birds singing.

You push the gate open and start to follow the little pathway in front you. It leads upwards through pretty flower borders on either side. Stop and take a look at the plants, inhale their scent and watch as the bees and butterflies visit them.

The winding pathway levels out, and you see a fork that takes you off to one side of the main path. You follow it as is spirals down to a sunken stone courtyard. With grey stone walls surrounding you and wide flagstones beneath your feet, in the centre is what looks like a round cover to a well. The cover is wooden but decorated with black wrought iron, the design depicts two interlocking circles.

There is a large iron ring on one side of the cover. You reach down and lift the lid open. It is heavy but you manage and the well lid props open.

Standing back, you notice several baskets of fresh flowers and greenery sat on the top of the surrounding wall. You are drawn to take them and start to decorate the edge of the well.

Starting with a circle of greenery and then lacing each flower in, until the well is crowned with a beautiful floral circlet.

Once you feel it is done, you sit on the edge of the wall admiring the well dressing you have created.

Take a moment now to give thanks for what you have in life, send out your gratitude.

When you are ready you reach into your pocket and draw out a coin, you throw it into the well and listen for it to hit the water in the dark depths below. Once you hear the tiny splash you make a wish.

Sit beside the well for some time now, allow your thoughts to drift wherever they may take you.

When you are ready to leave take a final look back at the well and head back up to the pathway.

Follow it back through the gardens and out to where you began.

Slowly and gently come back to the here and now.

Wriggle your fingers and toes and open your eyes.

Steam Room

Experiencing a sauna or stream room can be a cleansing and therapeutic experience, but it can also be uncomfortable if you have breathing issues. Visiting the steam room in a meditation gives you all the benefits without any problems.

Find a quiet place where you won't be disturbed and make yourself comfortable. Take a few deep breaths in and out.

As your world around you dissipates you find yourself in a forest, a dark green canopy overhead and trees all around you. Beneath your feet is a floor of bracken and fallen leaves.

Looking through the trees ahead of you there seems to be a structure so you head towards it.

As you draw nearer you see it is a round building constructed from light colour wood.

The door to the roundhouse swings open as you approach so you step inside.

It is very warm, but not stifling, just pleasant.

Inside is a bench with a folded towel and above it a coat hook. In front of you is another door with a window, you look through the glass.

The door leads to a steam room.

You feel the urge to undress, hanging your clothes on the peg and wrapping the towel around you.

Head through the door and into the steam room.

The air is hot and moist but not overwhelming.

The sides of the room are flanked with wooden benches. In the centre of the room stands a raised fire pit, full with smouldering charcoal and hot stones. Beside it sits a bucket of water with a ladle.

Take the ladle and scoop water from the bucket tipping it onto the hot coals. A cloud of steam erupts, and a hiss fills the air.

Take a seat on one of the benches and make yourself comfortable. Watch the steam as it rises and fills the room. Do you notice any particular shapes or images? There may be a message here for you. Take your time relaxing in the heat of the steam room.

Add more water to the coals when you feel the need and watch for any messages.

You begin to feel drowsy now, so you shake yourself and stand up. Head back out of the door to the entryway.

Remove the towel and dress yourself.

Open the outer door and step out into the fresh cool air.

Think about any images or messages you received.

When you are ready slowly and gently come back to the here and now.

Open your eyes and wriggle your fingers and toes.

Snow

There is nothing more beautiful and peaceful than a blanket of freshly laid snow. But it only happens at certain times of the year and in certain places. Using the medium of meditation you can experience the magic of snow at any time.

Find a quiet place where you won't be disturbed and make yourself comfortable. Take a few deep breaths in and out.

As your world around you dissipates you find yourself on the side of a mountain, the landscape as far as the eye can see is covered in a blanket of soft freshly laid white snow.

The air is cool and crisp, and the sky is a clear blue. You are not cold, as you are dressed to suit the weather.

Take a few deep breathes in and out, feel the fresh air hit your lungs. Watch the mist as you breathe out and your breath hits the cold air.

Listen to the silence, that special quiet that only a fresh snow fall brings.

Then begin to walk, each footstep making a soft crunch as you proceed. There is no direction, allow your intuition to take you where it wants to go. Take in the landscape as you walk. The snow-covered trees and mountains, the slopes and dips all wearing their white blanket.

Stop and turn, look back along the way you have come. See the tracks you have made in the snow. Are they in a straight line or a winding zig zag trail? This is your past, take some time to think about how far you have come and what you have achieved.

Now turn and look ahead. The way before you is a blank canvas, open and full of opportunity and possibilities. Ask yourself where do you want it to take you?

Take some time to think about your plans for the future.

Next reach down and scoop up a handful of snow. Mould it together into a ball and speak your desire into the sphere of snow.

Now throw it ahead of you, as far as you can. Watch it travel through the air and then land.

You have put your plans into action.

Take a long look around the landscape once more, the land of snowy opportunity. Remember your plans and know that you need to follow through with them.

When you are ready, slowly and gently come back to the here and now.

Open your eyes and wriggle your fingers and toes.

The Ocean

I am lucky enough to live close by the sea, it is the place I visit when I need to release, unwind and recuperate. The ocean has a very calming and restorative energy to it. You can achieve a similar experience with meditation.

Find a quiet place where you won't be disturbed and make yourself comfortable. Take a few deep breaths in and out.

As your world around you dissipates you find yourself standing on a sandy shoreline. It is dusk. In front of you is the ocean, the waves gently lapping at your feet. The sky is a beautiful canvas of oranges, yellows and blues as the sun appears to be dipping into the water on the horizon.

Sit down on the soft sand and make yourself comfortable. Watch as the sun slowly sets, heading down beneath the watery horizon.

As you watch, allow the sun to take away and worries, fears or negative energy that you are holding onto. Let the sunset remove those, taking them down with it as it sets.

Visualise the negative energy being drawn away from you and taken down into the water. If you prefer you can whisper, say out loud or shout with the things you want to get rid of.

The sky now fills with a sparkle of stars, tiny dots of precious light scattered across an inky blue background.

You feel calm and relaxed.

Watch the waves now, as they creep closer in over the sand. Each wave bringing fresh white foam and splashes of water with it.

The ocean can bring you positive energy, wishes, hopes and desires. Tell the water what you need.

Each wave coming in to bring you happy, positive energy full of opportunity and new ventures.

Sit quietly and let the waves help you.

When you are ready stand up and send your thanks to the sunset and the ocean.

Slowly and gently come back to the here and now.

Open your eyes and wriggle your fingers and toes.

White Springs

On the other side of the road from the Chalice Well Gardens in Glastonbury stands an old Victorian pump house that is fed by a natural spring. It is a very special place that has a unique energy. Work with this meditation to make a connection.

Find a quiet place where you won't be disturbed and make yourself comfortable. Take a few deep breaths in and out.

As your world around you dissipates you find yourself standing in a narrow roadway that leads up towards a grassy green tor. In the very distance you can see the remains of a stone turret standing on top of the hill.

To your right is a small courtyard with a low stone wall surrounding it. Pots of pretty flowers flank the wall at the back. To your left is a tap in the wall, with a stone trough beneath.

Beside the trough is a blue wooden door, which is standing ajar.

Go to the trough of water and put your hands in, lifting a scoop of fresh water up to your face. Feel the cool refreshing water on your skin.

Listening carefully, you can hear the strains of a singing bowl dancing along on the air. You look up and realise it is coming from behind the blue door.

Standing up you head towards the door and push it open, stepping inside.

It is dark and it takes a moment for your eyes to adjust.

There are candles lit, lots of them on every surface, on walls and floors all around the inside of the spring. The floor is a grey stone as are the walls around you.

In the centre of the room there appears to be a low circular stone wall holding a pool of water.

On several of the surrounding walls are stone altars, adorned with candles, ornaments and offerings of all kinds.

At one end is a wooden framework built from long twigs and twisted branches forming a canopy. You enter and inside are benches on either side with an altar at the far end. There is a bowl filled with fresh flower petals, pick some up and place them in the centre of the altar as an offering. Give you thanks for the opportunity of being in the white springs. Take some time here.

When you are ready turn and walk towards the pool in the centre of the room.

Sit on the wall that surrounds it and trail your hand in the water. You shiver as the water is icy cold.

Take off your shoes and swing your legs around letting them slide into the water as you sit on the wall. The water is so cold but fills you with a clarity and focus. The water is not deep, you can stand, and it comes halfway up you calves. Walk across the pool. Each step brings you more clarity of thought, clearing your mind from clutter and any worries you might have.

Now walk around the pool, in a circle, mindful of each step allowing you to release and let go that which no longer serves you. On your next lap around the pool allow the water to impart any wisdom or messages that it feels you need. Each step also imbuing you with positive energy.

When you are ready come back to the side of the pool. Sit quietly here for as long as you want.

Now slowly swing your legs back over the side, put on your shoes and send your thanks to the water.

Walk back to the blue door and step out into the sunshine again.

Turn and give your thanks once again to the energy of the white springs.

Slowly and gently come back to the here and now.

Open your eyes and wriggle your fingers and toes.

Rain

I don't think there is anything more cleansing and releasing than standing in a shower of rain. You are tapping into Mother Nature's energy from the source. If you don't fancy getting soaking wet in reality, then a meditation can help.

Find a quiet place where you won't be disturbed and make yourself comfortable. Take a few deep breaths in and out.

As your world around you dissipates you find yourself standing in a field, lush green grass beneath your feet and as far as the eye can see around you.

You are wearing a loose cotton garment and your feet are bare.

The sky above you is a dark grey and filled with storm clouds.

Small spots of rain start to fall, turn your face upwards towards the sky and feel them on your skin.

Light rain at first, you throw your arms out wide and let the droplets fall onto you, welcoming the refreshing and cleansing energy.

The rain begins to get heavier, visualise it clearing out negative energy, bad habits and thoughts or ideas you no longer wish to hang onto.

Each droplet of rain working to cleanse and clear.

Feel the rain on your skin, your hair and your body as it works to release.

Start walking or even running across the field, you have the freedom to go wherever you please, bathing in the fresh rain.

Run, dance, shout, spin around in circles – be free!

Then drop, lay down on the wet ground and relax looking up to the sky.

The rain slows, not so heavy now, only just a few light drops, until it stops completely.

Allow your body to connect to the earth beneath you, grounding and centering your energy.

You are cleansed and relaxed.

When you are ready, slowly and gently come back to the here and now.

Open your eyes and wriggle your fingers and toes.

The Mists

Mist or fog has a very magical energy to it. It shrouds and hides but then reveals its secrets. Allow this meditation to reveal the truth to you.

Find a quiet place where you won't be disturbed and make yourself comfortable. Take a few deep breaths in and out.

As the world around you dissipates you find yourself standing on a riverbank. It is early morning, and the dew is still on the grass.

In front of you the river is wide and running strong and fast. As you look across the river you cannot make out the other side as it is shrouded in mist.

At the edge of the river on your side of the bank is a small wooden boat.

Making your way down to the edge you step carefully into the vessel and sit down. The boat does not seem to have any oars or means of propulsion. But you need not worry, as soon as you are comfortable the boat starts moving, slowly and gently of its own accord.

It turns from the riverbank and sets out across the wide river.

You can feel the dampness of the mist in the air on your skin. Birds call out from unseen trees and animals splash around in the water further downstream, hidden from your view.

As the boat drifts across the water, you find yourself thinking of a question, a situation or an issue that you need clarity on. Something that you would like to find the truth about or an answer to.

Looking ahead of you, as the boat continues on its journey the mist begins to clear, slowly and gradually. The other side of the river starts to become clear.

Allow your thoughts to be open to any messages that the mist may bring to you.

Gently the boat reaches the other side of the river, the mist now gone completely.

Carefully you step outside of the boat and onto the land.

There is something in front of you, a message, an object, a person. Something that will give you clarity and answers.

Look and listen.

Spend some time here making sure you understand the meaning.

When you are ready turn and look back across the river, the mists have cleared, and you can see perfectly back to the other side.

You have your answer.

When you are ready slowly and gently come back to the here and now.

Open your eyes and wriggle your fingers and toes.

Lake

A lake is still and calming and can provide a reflective surface for you to seek symbols, images and ultimately insight.

Find a quiet place where you won't be disturbed and make yourself comfortable. Take a few deep breaths in and out.

As the world around you dissipates you find yourself standing in a valley. Mountains covered with rocks and lush grass rise above you on either side. Around you are sparse pine trees, which have covered the floor with their dried pine needles and pinecones.

In front of you is a large lake, it stretches from one side of the valley right across to the other and reaches back as far as you can see.

The water is lapping gently and calmly against the shoreline.

You walk forward and meet it at the water's edge.

Sit down and make yourself comfortable.

Gazing out across the lake, ask a question or seek guidance for something.

Listen to the gentle sound of the water as it reaches the shoreline. Soft and gentle.

Allow the rhythmic sound to wash over you.

Watch for any symbols or images on the surface of the water.

Keep an eye out for any water creatures or birds too, they may have a message for you.

Sit for as long as you need to.

When you are ready, stand up and take a last look around the valley and across the water.

Gently and slowly come back to the here and now.

Waterfall

Waterfalls are beautiful to watch and to listen to. There is a wonderful ancient power to the water cascading downwards.

Find a quiet place where you won't be disturbed and make yourself comfortable. Take a few deep breaths in and out.

As the world around you dissipates you find yourself in a tropical forest, lush undergrown beneath your feet and a large canopy of deep green above your head. Stand and listen to all the sounds of wildlife and the forest around you.

There seems to be a small pathway ahead, so you walk along it. Look around you as you walk, at the forest, the floor and the canopy above.

The pathway leads you through a gap in the trees and you step out into the sunlight and a bright clearing.

A sound of crashing water meets your ears, and you look up to see an enormous waterfall ahead. Streams of water cascading down from the rocks above into a bright blue pool below.

You make your way towards it.

Walking around the edge of the pool you notice how beautifully clear the water is. As you reach the waterfall you realise there is a gap, and you can carefully walk behind the water. As you do so, you find there is a large cave that opens up right behind the cascading water.

Inside the cave it is damp and misty from the water but the view outwards through the sheet of water coming down is amazing.

There are rocks inside the cave, so you sit yourself down on one of them. Listen to the sound of the water and watch as it tumbles downwards.

What can that water help you with? What can it remove from you, that no longer serves? Speak into the waterfall, ask it to remove those things that you no longer want or need.

Let the water snatch away those memories, emotions and energies and throw them downwards, away from you.

Sit here for as long as you feel you need to.

When you are ready, make your way back out of the cave and down to the edge of the pool.

Now sit beside the pool and look into the water, visualise positive energy and good things to replace those that you have released.

When you are ready stand up and make your way back into the forest again.

Then gently and slowly come back to the here and now.

Fountain

Fountains make me think of grand stately homes and mansions. Huge stone designs with ornate features and waterspouts. They can be very useful for cleansing and purifying.

Find a quiet place where you won't be disturbed and make yourself comfortable. Take a few deep breaths in and out.

As the world around you dissipates you find yourself standing at the end of a smart path with regimented clipped yew bushes running either side and rose bushes laid out in geometric patterns behind them.

In front of you is an imposing building, a stately home perhaps?

Just in front of what looks like the main doorway, with its stone pillars either side is a large foundation.

You walk slowly along the path, admiring the rose bushes either side until you reach the fountain.

The fountain has a stone surround wide enough to sit on, the centre rises up with ornate dolphins twisting together with their heads towards the sky, spouting great plumes of water up into the air.

You look down into the water and notice the inside is decorated with a beautiful watery mosaic design.

Sit yourself down on the side of the fountain.

You feel the urge to remove your shoes and socks, and then swing yourself around and place your feet into the cool water of the fountain pool.

Immediately you feel calm and relaxed. The cool water easing any tension and stress.

You sit quietly and look properly at the mosaic on the bottom of the fountain. What images do you see, what patterns have been created?

Stay seated with your feet in the cool water for as long as you wish.

When you are ready swing your legs back around but stay seated.

Allow the warm air to dry your legs and your feet, feel the sun on your skin bringing positive energy.

When you are ready, slowly and gently come back to the here and now.

Exercise

Take a look at the water places mentioned here. Do some research in your local area and see how many of these types of places you can find or even visit. Keep notes on your experiences.

Practical Water Elements

Herbs and Plants

Each plant has an association or correspondence with one of the elements. Often it is based upon the magical or medicinal properties of the plant. You can work with the plant in meditation or use the actual item as an ingredient in incense or spell work. Here is a basic list of plants and herbs that correspond to the element of water to get you started:

African Violet Magical Properties:
Protection, spirituality, blessings, happiness
Ruling planet – Venus
Element – Water
Gender – Feminine

Alexanders Magical Properties:
Sea magic, intuition, emotions, cleansing, releasing
Element – Water
Gender – Masculine

Aloe Magical Properties:
Luck, protection, calming, moon magic, psychic abilities
Ruling planet – Moon, Saturn
Sign – Sagittarius
Element – Water
Gender – Feminine

Ash Magical Properties:
Protection, prosperity, dispels negativity, improves health, sea magic, dreams, love, intuition
Ruling planet – Sun and Neptune
Element – Fire and Water

Gender – Masculine

Aster Magical Properties:
Love, consecration, protection, Goddess, lost items
Ruling planet – Venus
Sign – Libra
Element – Water
Gender – Feminine

Belladonna Magical Properties:
Astral travel, baneful spells, Crone magic
Ruling planet – Saturn, Mars
Element – Water
Gender – Feminine

Birch Magical Properties:
Purification, protection, exorcism, new beginnings, courage, fertility, love, release
Ruling planet – Venus, Moon, Jupiter
Sign – Sagittarius
Element – Water, Air
Gender – Feminine

Bladder wrack Magical Properties:
Protection, sea magic, money, psychic powers, weather magic
Ruling planet – Moon
Sign – Pisces
Element – Water
Gender – Feminine

Bleeding Heart Magical Properties:
Love
Ruling planet – Venus

Element – Water
Gender – Feminine

Bluebell Heart Magical Properties:
Truth, shape shifting, protection, healing
Ruling planet – Mercury
Element – Water
Gender – Feminine

Burdock Magical Properties:
Protection, healing, cleansing
Ruling planet – Venus
Sign – Leo, Libra
Element – Water
Gender – Feminine

Calamus Magical Properties:
Money, protection, healing, luck
Ruling planet – Moon, Sun
Element – Water
Gender – Feminine

Camellia Magical Properties:
Abundance, prosperity, spirituality
Ruling planet – Moon
Element – Water
Gender – Feminine

Catnip Magical Properties:
Love, fertility, cat magic, dreams, happiness, courage
Ruling planet – Venus
Sign – Cancer, Libra
Element – Water
Gender – Feminine

Chamomile Magical Properties:
Sleep, dreams, love, calm, money, relaxation, purification, balancing
Ruling planet – Sun
Sign – Leo
Element – Water
Gender – Masculine

Chickweed Magical Properties:
Love, fidelity, dreams, protection, fertility, moon magic
Ruling planet – Moon
Element – Water
Gender – Feminine

Coltsfoot Magical Properties:
Visions, love, energy, health, tranquillity, peace
Ruling planet – Venus
Sign – Taurus
Element – Water
Gender – Feminine

Columbine/Aquilegia Magical Properties:
Love, courage, faeries, clarity, jealousy
Ruling planet – Venus
Element – Water, Air
Gender – Feminine

Comfrey Magical Properties:
Money, travel, protection, healing, hex breaking, bringing together
Ruling planet – Saturn
Sign – Capricorn
Element – Water
Gender – Feminine

Cornflower/Batchelor's Buttons Magical Properties:
Love, psychic powers, protection, fertility, abundance, Faeries
Ruling planet – Venus, Saturn
Element – Water, Earth
Gender – Feminine

Cowslip Magical Properties:
Healing, peace, calm, treasure, youth, anti-visitor
Ruling planet – Venus
Sign –Aries, Scorpio
Element – Water
Gender – Feminine

Crocus Magical Properties:
Love, happiness, hope, visions, blessings, new beginnings
Ruling planet – Venus
Sign – Aquarius
Element – Water
Gender – Feminine

Cyclamen Magical Properties:
Happiness, self-esteem, protection, fertility, love, lust, nightmares
Ruling planet – Venus
Element – Water
Gender – Feminine

Daffodil Magical Properties:
Luck, fertility, protection, love, exorcism
Ruling planet – Venus
Sign – Leo
Element – Water
Gender – Feminine

Daisy Magical Properties:
Love, lust, protection, happiness, dreams, strength, courage
Ruling planet – Venus
Sign – Cancer, Taurus
Element – Water
Gender – Feminine

Delphinium Magical Properties:
Protection, midsummer, faeries, dragons
Ruling planet – Venus
Element – Water
Gender – Feminine

Dittany of Crete Magical Properties:
Love, spirit work, visions, protection
Ruling planet – Venus
Element – Water
Gender – Feminine

Dulse Magical Properties:
Lust, love, harmony, peace, protection
Ruling planet – Moon
Sign – Pisces
Element – Water
Gender – Feminine

Elder Magical Properties:
Protection, healing, faeries, purification, intuition, exorcism, hex breaking, rebirth
Ruling planet – Venus
Sign – Sagittarius, Aquarius, Libra
Element – Water
Gender – Feminine

Eucalyptus Magical Properties:
Moon magic, sun magic, divination, dreams, healing, purification
Ruling planet – Moon, Sun
Element – Water, Air
Gender – Feminine

Evening Primrose Magical Properties:
Feminine energy, Moon magic, faerie, hunting
Ruling planet – Moon
Element – Water
Gender – Feminine

Feverfew Magical Properties:
Protection, peace, health, purification
Ruling planet – Venus
Sign – Aries, Sagittarius, Libra
Element – Water
Gender – Masculine

Foxglove Magical Properties:
Protection, gossip, faeries, divination
Ruling planet – Venus, Saturn
Element – Water
Gender – Feminine

Geranium (Pelargonium) Magical Properties:
Protection, fertility, love, socialise, aura cleansing
Ruling planet – Venus
Sign – Pisces
Element – Water
Gender – Feminine

Gourd Magical Properties:
Protection, cleansing
Ruling planet – Moon
Element – Water
Gender – Masculine

Heather Magical Properties:
Luck, protection, cleansing, ghosts, rain, spirit, love, friendship, faeries, dreams, shape shifting
Ruling planet – Venus
Element – Water
Gender – Feminine

Hyacinth Magical Properties:
Love, happiness, peace, sleep, nightmares, abundance
Ruling planet – Venus
Element – Water
Gender – Feminine

Iris Magical Properties:
Wisdom, purification, moon magic, divination, dreams, love
Ruling planet – Moon, Venus
Sign – Taurus, Aquarius
Element – Water
Gender – Feminine

Ivy Magical Properties:
Protection, healing, binding, love, abundance, fidelity
Ruling planet – Saturn, Moon
Sign – Scorpio
Element – Water
Gender – Feminine

Jasmine Magical Properties:
Dreams, money, love, meditation, lust
Ruling planet – Moon, Venus
Sign – Cancer
Element – Water
Gender – Feminine

Lady's Mantle Magical Properties:
Love
Ruling planet – Venus
Sign – Scorpio
Element – Water
Gender – Feminine

Lemon Balm Magical Properties:
Success, healing, anti-depression, memory, love, anxiety
Ruling planet – Moon & Venus
Sign – Cancer
Element – Water
Gender – Feminine

Lilac Magical Properties:
Protection, exorcism, love, meditation
Ruling planet – Venus
Element – Water
Gender – Feminine

Lily Magical Properties:
Goddess, witchcraft, hexes, uncrossing, protection
Ruling planet – Moon, Venus
Sign – Scorpio
Element – Water
Gender – Feminine

Lobelia Magical Properties:
Love, weather magic, protection, purification
Ruling planet – Saturn, Neptune
Element – Water
Gender – Feminine

Mallow Magical Properties:
Love, Samhain, protection
Ruling planet – Moon, Venus
Element – Water
Gender – Feminine

Myrrh Magical Properties:
Protection, purification, healing, Crone, Underworld, courage
Ruling planet – Mars, Sun
Sign – Aries, Aquarius
Element – Water
Gender – Feminine

Myrtle Magical Properties:
Love, protection, money
Ruling planet – Venus, Moon
Sign – Taurus
Element – Water
Gender – Feminine

Oak Magical Properties:
Healing, health, protection, money, fertility, luck, strength, vitality, power
Ruling planet – Sun, Jupiter, Mars
Sign – Sagittarius
Element – Fire, Water

Gender – Masculine

Orchid Magical Properties:
Spirituality, love, abundance
Ruling planet – Venus
Element – Water
Gender – Feminine

Pansy Magical Properties:
Love, rain magic, focus, rebirth
Ruling planet – Saturn, Venus
Element – Water
Gender – Feminine

Passionflower Magical Properties:
Love, calm, peace, sleep, friendship
Ruling planet – Venus
Element – Water
Gender – Feminine

Periwinkle Magical Properties:
Money, protection, love, lust, mental powers, Goddess, purification, spirit
Ruling planet – Venus
Element – Water
Gender – Feminine

Poppy Magical Properties:
Love, sleep, money, luck, fertility, rebirth, grief
Ruling planet – Moon, Mars, Venus
Sign – Capricorn
Element – Water
Gender – Feminine

Rose Magical Properties:
Love, psychic powers, healing, luck, protection, peace, mysteries, knowledge, dreams, friendship, death and rebirth, abundance
Ruling planet – Venus, Moon
Sign – Pisces
Element – Water
Gender – Feminine

Sandalwood (Red) Magical Properties:
Meditation, love
Ruling planet – Venus, Jupiter
Sign – Sagittarius, Virgo
Element – Water
Gender – Feminine

Sandalwood (White) Magical Properties:
Death rites, purification, wishes, psychic powers
Ruling planet – Moon, Mercury
Sign – Sagittarius, Virgo
Element – Water
Gender – Feminine

Self-Heal Magical Properties:
Releasing, cleansing, spirituality, stress, calming, clarity, protection
Ruling planet – Venus
Element – Water
Gender – Feminine

Scullcap Magical Properties:
Faithfulness, restoring, prosperity, stress, peace
Ruling planet – Saturn
Sign – Virgo

Element – Water
Gender – Feminine

Sea Holly Magical Properties:
Travel, peace, love
Ruling planet – Venus
Element – Water
Gender – Feminine

Solomon's Seal Magical Properties:
Wisdom, knowledge, protection, exorcism, success, Elementals, purification
Ruling planet – Saturn
Sign – Capricorn
Element – Water
Gender – Feminine

Sweetgrass Magical Properties:
Cleansing, purification, wishes, protection, uplifting
Planet – Venus
Element – Air, Water

Sweet pea Magical Properties:
Courage, strength, friendship, peace, happiness, truth, spirituality, psychic abilities, protection, sleep
Ruling planet – Venus, Moon, Mercury
Element – Water
Gender – Feminine

Tansy Magical Properties:
Health, longevity, rebirth, cleansing, protection, travel
Ruling planet – Venus
Sign – Gemini
Element – Water

Gender – Feminine

Thyme Magical Properties:
Healing, health, peace, psychic powers, love, purification, courage, releasing, sleep, beauty
Ruling planet – Venus
Sign – Gemini, Taurus, Libra
Element – Water
Gender – Feminine

Valerian Magical Properties:
Protection, purification, love, sleep, peace, animal spirit, stress
Ruling planet – Venus, Jupiter
Sign – Virgo
Element – Water, Earth
Gender – Feminine

Violet Magical Properties:
Love, lust, peace, healing, protection, commitment, death and rebirth
Ruling planet – Venus
Sign – Cancer, Libra
Element – Water
Gender – Feminine

Willow Magical Properties:
Love, protection, healing, cleansing, wishes, release, inspiration, intuition
Ruling planet – Moon
Sign – Pisces
Element – Water
Gender – Feminine

Yarrow Magical Properties:
Psychic powers, love, courage, exorcism, dreams, peace, happiness, divination, protection.
Ruling planet – Venus
Element – Water
Gender – Feminine

Yew Magical Properties:
Death and rebirth, transformation, astral travel, ancient knowledge, knowledge
Ruling planet – Saturn, Mercury
Element – Water, Earth
Gender – Feminine

Incense

Incense can be a loose mixture burnt on charcoal or by lighting incense cones and sticks. Incense is used to clear negative energy, create sacred space, complement spell work or add energy to a ritual. If you can't use incense for health reasons you could try using essential oil on a burner or scented candles. I often pop loose incense onto the top of an oil burner with a tea light underneath. The heat warms the blend and disperses the scent but doesn't give off any smoke. Incense is used frequently to cleanse, whether it is by passing the item through the smoke of the incense itself or by using incense to smudge something – your home, your body or an item. To smudge, you light your incense and waft the smoke around your body or into each room in your home. Send the smoke into all the corners of your house and any area you wish to purify. The power of the smoke cleanses and purifies. Loose incense can also be used in spell pouches and witch bottles but also to draw sigils or symbols with. I start with a tree resin base such as frankincense or copal. Add in something woody to help it burn longer and then dried herbs and spices. To boost the scent, you can add a few drops of essential oil to the mixture.

Some water element incense blends
Use equal parts of each ingredient.

Incense #1
Geranium
Lemon Balm
Jasmine
Myrrh

Incense #2
Lemon
Lemon balm
Rose
Sandalwood (white)

Incense #3
Thyme
Yarrow
Heather
Chamomile
Myrrh

Incense #4
Cardamom
Grapefruit
Camellia
Vanilla

Exercise
Keep a note of any blends that you create and write up how each one worked. It is useful to keep a record for future blends.

Essential Oils

An essential oil is a concentrated essence of the plant. The oil is extracted from either the seeds, the peel, the resin, leaves, roots, bark or flowers. Essential oils have been used for thousands of years in religious ceremonies, for anointing, filling a room with fragrance, in foods and perfumes and for healing and well-being. When purchasing essential oils do make sure they are pure and not mixed with chemicals or 'watered down'. Some of the oils can be expensive but remember that you only use a few drops at a time so they will last.

Oil blends are useful for dressing candles for spell work, picking a corresponding oil to your intent and rubbing the candle with the oil. Or adding to your own bath water for a ritual bath or using to anoint yourself before ritual. Oil blends can also be added to an oil burner, I pop a piece of wax into the top first then add the oil, it stops it from burning. Please test a drop or two on a small area of your skin before you go slapping on loads of oil, just in case you are allergic to it. NEVER put essential oil straight onto your skin, always mix it into a base oil first.

A useful method for breathing in essential oils is to create your oil blend then add it to a jar containing a couple of tablespoons of coarse sea salt. Mix together and pop a lid on the jar. Then when you feel the need, open the jar and take a couple of deep breaths.

Oil blends are easy to make, and you can use any type of base oil such as almond oil, jojoba oil, apricot kernel oil, coconut oil, even olive oil. Then add a few drops of essential oil in whatever blends you want. If you are experimenting with blends, I would suggest using pieces of card to test the scent on first. Put a drop of each essential oil on a small slip of card (or paper towel) add the next oil and sniff to see if you like it, then add the next drop etc. Then you won't end up ruining a whole bottle of base oil by adding in random essential oils.

For a blend to use in an oil burner, bath or diffuser you can create a blend without using a base oil. Any blend you are intending to use on your skin for anointing or massage NEEDS to be diluted with a base oil. As a general rule of thumb, I would use 10ml of base oil to 20-25 drops of essential oil.

Some water essential oil blends

Oil blend #1
Lemon
Grapefruit
Rose

Oil blend #2
Chamomile
Thyme
Violet

Oil blend #3
Willow
Hyacinth

Oil blend #4
Cyclamen
Evening Primrose
Lilac

Exercise
Keep a note of any blends that you create and write up how each one worked. It is useful to keep a record for future blends.

Magical Food
Just as each plant or herb has magical properties, so does food. Use them as offerings, eat to absorb the magic or use in spell

working. Here are some foods that correspond to the element of water:

Apple Magical Properties:
Love, healing, clarity, knowledge, abundance, spirit work
Ruling planet – Venus
Element – Water
Gender – Feminine

Apricot Magical Properties:
Peace, love, passion, romance
Ruling planet – Venus
Element – Water
Gender – Feminine

Blackberries Magical Properties:
Prosperity, protection, fertility, Faerie
Ruling planet – Venus
Element – Water, Fire, Earth
Gender – Feminine

Blueberries Magical Properties:
Calm, peace, protection, passion, fertility
Ruling planet – Moon
Element – Earth, water
Gender – Feminine

Broccoli Magical Properties:
Strength, protection
Ruling planet – Moon
Element – Water
Gender – Feminine

Brussels Sprouts Magical Properties:
Stability, endurance, protection
Ruling planet – Moon
Element – Water
Gender – Feminine

Cabbage Magical Properties:
Moon magic, protection, prosperity, fertility, love
Ruling planet – Moon
Element – Water
Gender – Feminine

Cardamom Magical Properties:
Love, passion, clarity, uplifting, protection
Ruling planet – Venus, Mars
Element – Water
Gender – Feminine

Cauliflower Magical Properties:
Emotions, moon magic, protection
Ruling planet – Moon
Element – Water
Gender – Feminine

Caviar Magical Properties:
Emotions, passion
Ruling planet – Moon
Element – Water
Gender – Feminine

Celery Magical Properties:
Clarity, passion, peace
Ruling planet – Mercury

Element – Fire, Water, Air
Gender – Masculine

Cherry Magical Properties:
Love, fertility, divination, beginnings
Ruling planet – Venus
Element – Water, Air
Gender – Feminine

Coconut Magical Properties:
Protection, purification, chastity
Ruling planet – Moon
Element – Water
Gender – Feminine

Coffee Magical Properties:
Energy, clarity, divination
Ruling planet – Mars
Element – Fire, Water
Gender – Feminine

Crab Magical Properties:
Spirituality, hex breaking
Ruling planet – Moon
Element – Water
Gender – Feminine

Cranberry Magical Properties:
Protection, emotions, communication
Ruling planet – Mars
Element – Water, Fire
Gender – Feminine

Cucumber Magical Properties:
Fertility, emotions, chastity, meditation, spirituality, purification, healing
Ruling planet – Moon
Element – Water
Gender – Feminine

Eggs Magical Properties:
Fertility, creation, life, new beginnings, divination
Element – Water, Earth, Air, Fire
Gender – Masculine/Feminine

Fish Magical Properties:
Fertility, Prosperity, Abundance, healing, emotions, cleansing, purification
Element – Water
Gender – Feminine

Game Magical Properties:
Fidelity, divination, power, energy
Element – Fire, Air, Earth, Water
Gender – Masculine

Grapefruit Magical Properties:
Happiness, spirit work, purification, depression, energy
Ruling planet – Jupiter, Sun
Element – Fire, Water
Gender – Feminine

Grapes Magical Properties:
Spiritual, fertility, moon magic
Ruling planet – Moon
Element – Air, Water

Gender – Feminine

Gravy Magical Properties:
Calming, emotions, healing, cleansing, purification
Ruling planet – Moon
Element – Water
Gender – Feminine

Honey Magical Properties:
Happiness, healing, love, prosperity, passion, spirituality, faerie
Element – Water, Earth
Gender – Feminine

Ice Cream Magical Properties:
Love, spirituality, various depending on what flavours you add
Ruling planet – Moon
Element – Water
Gender – Feminine

Kiwi Fruit Magical Properties:
Love, romance
Ruling planet – Moon
Element – Water, Earth
Gender – Masculine

Lemon Magical Properties:
Purification, moon magic, happiness, decisions, uplifting, love, protection, friendship, fidelity
Ruling planet – Moon
Element – Water
Gender – Feminine

Lettuce Magical Properties:
Fertility, meditation, astral travel, calm
Ruling planet – Moon
Element – Water
Gender – neutral

Liquorice Magical Properties:
Love, passion, balance
Ruling planet – Venus, Mercury
Element – Earth, Water
Gender – Fcminine

Lobster Magical Properties:
Sea magic, power, courage
Element – Water, Fire
Gender – Masculine

Maple Syrup Magical Properties:
Love, money, attraction, positive energy, healing, binding
Ruling planet – Jupiter
Element – Earth, Water
Gender – Masculine & Feminine

Margarine Magical Properties:
Various depending on the vegetable oil used
Element – Water

Melon Magical Properties:
Love, chaos, healing, purification
Ruling planet – Moon
Element – Water
Gender – Feminine

Milk Magical Properties:
Feminine power, goddess energy, moon magic, nurturing, offerings, love, spirituality, Faeries
Ruling planet – Moon
Element – Water
Gender – Feminine

Nectarine Magical Properties:
Love
Ruling planet – Venus
Element – Water
Gender – Feminine

Oils Magical Properties:
Various depending on the type of vegetable
Element – Water

Oyster Magical Properties:
Passion, balance
Ruling planet – Moon
Element – Water
Gender – Masculine & feminine

Papaya Magical Properties:
Love, protection
Ruling planet – Moon
Element – Water
Gender –Feminine

Passion Fruit Magical Properties:
Love, peace, friendship, meditation, dreams
Ruling planet – Venus
Element – Water
Gender – Feminine

Peach Magical Properties:
Love, fertility, spirituality, wishes, longevity
Ruling planet – Venus
Element – Water, Air
Gender – Feminine

Pear Magical Properties:
Passion, love, prosperity, luck
Ruling planet – Venus
Element – Water, Air
Gender – Feminine

Peas Magical Properties:
Love
Ruling planet – Venus
Element – Water
Gender – Feminine

Plum Magical Properties:
Love, spirituality, relaxation, passion, longevity, wisdom, rebirth
Ruling planet – Venus
Element – Water, Air
Gender – Feminine

Raspberry Magical Properties:
Love, protection, strength
Ruling planet – Venus
Element – Water, Earth
Gender – Feminine

Strawberry Magical Properties:
Love, fertility, romance, luck, success
Ruling planet – Venus

Element – Water, Earth
Gender – Feminine

Sugar Magical Properties:
Love, protection
Ruling planet – Venus
Element – Water
Gender – Feminine

Sweet Potato Magical Properties:
Love, passion
Ruling planet – Venus
Element – Earth, Water
Gender – Feminine

Thyme Magical Properties:
Healing, health, peace, psychic powers, love, purification, courage, releasing, sleep, beauty
Ruling planet – Venus
Element – Water
Gender – Feminine

Tomato Magical Properties:
Love, passion, protection, creativity
Ruling planet – Venus
Element – Water
Gender – Feminine

Vanilla Magical Properties:
Love, spirituality, sex magic, passion, creativity
Ruling planet – Venus
Element – Water, Air
Gender – Feminine

Watercress Magical Properties:
Clarity, protection, fertility
Ruling planet – Mars
Element – Fire, Water
Gender – Feminine

Yogurt Magical Properties:
Spirituality, creativity, depression
Ruling planet – Moon
Element – Water, Air
Gender – Feminine

Water Recipes

With sugar, milk, vanilla and eggs all covering the element of water, it just lends itself to baking (I don't need an excuse really). These are a few of my favourite water element recipes.

Coconut Milk Cake

A delicious coconut cake that uses both shredded coconut and coconut milk – a double whammy of coconut flavour.

400g/14 oz sugar
225g/8 oz butter, room temperature
4 eggs, separated
90g/3 oz desiccated or shredded coconut
300g/10 ½ oz plain/all-purpose flour
2 tablespoons baking powder (yes, tablespoons!)
1 teaspoon salt
1 400ml/14 oz can coconut milk

- Preheat your oven to 350F/180C/Gas 4.
- Grease a Bundt tin. Don't skip this part otherwise the cake won't turn out properly.

- Beat the sugar, butter and egg yolks until smooth and creamy.
- Add in the shredded coconut.
- Whisk in the flour, baking powder, salt and coconut milk into the mix.
- In a separate bowl whisk the egg whites until they form soft peaks. Fold the egg whites into the cake batter.
- Pour the batter into the prepared tin.
- Bake in the oven for about 45 minutes, until a skewer inserted into the centre comes out clean.

Lemon Cookies

These melt in the mouth cookies have the lovely flavour of lemon to boost them.

170g/6 oz plain/all-purpose flour
50g/1 ½ oz cornflour/corn starch
Zest and juice of one lemon (approx. 2 tablespoons juice and 1 tablespoon zest)
Pinch salt
185g/6 ½ oz butter, room temperature
60g/2 oz icing/confectioner sugar

- Line a large baking sheet with baking parchment.
- Beat the butter and sugar until light and fluffy.
- Mix the flour, cornflour, zest and salt together in a separate bowl.
- Add the flour mix to the butter/sugar and stir to combine, bring it together to form a slightly sticky dough. If the mix is too sticky add a tablespoon of flour.
- Pop the dough onto a sheet of baking parchment and roll into a log shape. Place in the fridge for an hour to chill.
- Preheat your oven to 325F/170C/Gas 3.

- Remove the dough from the fridge and cut into ½" (1.3cm) slices.
- Place the slices onto the prepared baking sheet.
- Bake in the oven for 5 minutes, then raise the oven temperature to 350F/180C/Gas 4. Bake for a further 10 minutes.
- They should be light golden.
- Allow the cookies to cool on the baking sheet.

Cardamom & Lemon Muffins

Cardamon matches so well with lemon and who can resist a muffin?

165g/6 oz sugar
2 eggs
100ml/3 ½ fl oz vegetable oil
100ml/3 ½ fl oz milk
50ml/1 ¾ fl oz lemon juice
Zest of one lemon
1 teaspoon ground cardamom
300g/10 ½ oz plain/all-purpose flour
2 teaspoons baking powder
½ teaspoon bicarbonate soda
Pinch salt

- Preheat your oven to 350F/180C/Gas 4.
- Pop 12 muffin cases into a muffin tin.
- Mix the dry ingredients together and in a separate bowl whisk the wet ingredients together. Now fold the wet into the dry.
- Pour the batter into the muffin cases.
- Bake in the oven for 20-25 minutes until well risen and golden brown.

Options
Replace the lemon juice with orange juice.

Rice Pudding
One of my favourite dishes, it brings back so many childhood memories. Delicious for every day but add some poached plums and you have a fancy dessert for dinner parties too.

1 ½ pints/852 ml liquid – I make mine with 1-pint full fat milk and ½ pint evaporated milk, but you could also use double/heavy cream instead of the evaporated milk.
60g/2 oz caster sugar
1 piece star anise
1 teaspoon vanilla extract
130g/4 ½ oz arborio or basmati rice

- Pop the milk, cream/evap, sugar and vanilla into a saucepan. Stir over a medium heat until the sugar dissolves. Stir in the rice and bring to the boil, stirring occasionally. Add in the star anise.
- Reduce the heat to low and simmer for half an hour, stir occasionally. It should become a nice creamy mixture. Remove from the heat, cover with a lid and allow to stand for ten minutes. Serve warm or chilled.

Apple & Coconut Scones
The addition of coconut to the scone mixture gives it another dimension. Absolutely delicious served sliced with butter or if you are feeling indulgent add a dollop of cream too.

350g/12 ½ oz plain/all-purpose flour
3 teaspoons baking powder
Pinch salt

55g/2 oz sugar
100g/3 ½ oz butter, diced (cold)
1 apple, peeled, cored and grated
55g/2 oz desiccated coconut
100ml/3 ½ fl oz plain yoghurt
1 egg
1 teaspoon vanilla extract

- Preheat your oven to 200C/400F/Gas 6.
- Line a baking sheet with baking parchment.
- Pop the flour, baking powder, and sugar into a bowl. Add the butter and rub together until it resembles breadcrumbs. Add in the shredded apple and coconut. Mix to combine. Pour in the yogurt and egg – reserve a spoonful of the yogurt to brush the tops with.
- Stir the wet ingredients into the dry to bring it together to form a dough.
- Roll out on a floured surface to about 2.5cm/1" thick.
- Cut with a cookie cutter (I use a 2" wide cutter) and place on the prepared sheet.
- Brush the tops with the reserved yogurt.
- Bake in the oven for about 12 minutes, until nicely golden.

Crystals & Metals

Each crystal will have an association with one of the elements, sometimes more than one.

The basic fact is that crystals are taken from Mother Earth and some of the mining practices can be extremely harsh to the environment. Only you can make the decision about where you source your crystals from. There are some very good eco-friendly crystal providers, it may just take a bit of research on your part. A lot of crystal suppliers are now stating their sources which is very helpful.

If you want to connect with the element of water or use a water crystal in your spell working, then these are some suggestions of crystals to use:

Agate (Blue lace) magical properties:
Mediation, spirituality, uplifting, calming, peace, communication, emotions, support, optimism, happiness, protection, cleansing, healing, prosperity, longevity, strength, courage, clarity, success, patience, truth, stress, relaxation, creativity, justice, travel, renewal, understanding, soothing, trust

Energy	Receptive
Element	Water
Planet	Mercury
Zodiac	Gemini

Amethyst magical properties:
Peace, protection, success, good luck, hidden knowledge, legal issues, spirituality, contentment, soothing, relaxation, calm, hope, patience, transformation, changes, breaking patterns, grounding, guilt, overcoming addictions, business matters, judgement, clarity, courage, travel, psychic protection, sleep, anxiety, focus, understanding, happiness, justice, intuition, inspiration, channelling, meditation

Energy:	Receptive
Element:	Water
Planet:	Jupiter, Neptune
Zodiac:	Pisces, Scorpio, Sagittarius
Birthstone:	February

Celestite magical properties:
Divine, spirit work, love, clarity, decisions, meditation, communication, peace, dreams, stress, healing, astral travel, calming, uplifting, harmony, happiness, spirituality

Energy: Receptive
Element: Air, Water
Planet: Neptune, Venus
Zodiac: Gemini

Chrysocolla magical properties:
Wisdom, peace, patience, love, soothing, intuition, energy, calming, emotions, fear, strength, clarity, balance, negative energy, insight, releasing, spirituality, psychic abilities, guilt, divine, harmony, communication, meditation

Energy: Receptive
Element: Water
Planet: Venus
Zodiac: Taurus

Copper magical properties:
It provides support, co-operation, protection, love, attraction, purification, self-esteem, positive energy, communication, energy, psychic abilities, channelling, balance, understanding, harmony, money, confidence, optimism, divine connection, luck

Energy: Receptive
Element: Water
Planet: Venus
Zodiac: Taurus, Sagittarius

Fluorite magical properties:
Magic, imagination, discernment, aptitude, psychic protection, protection, purification, calming, relaxation, tension, anxiety, organisation, structure, challenges, declutter, releasing, support, breaking patterns, intuition, confidence, reassurance, comforting, communication, balance, spirituality, decisions, manifestation, peace, meditation, grounding, healing, cleansing, channelling, past

life work, fairy realm, amplifying, memory, power, emotions, depression, stability

Energy: Projective
Element: Water, Air
Planet: Neptune
Zodiac: Scorpio, Aquarius, Pisces

Jade magical properties:
Purification, harmony, friendship, luck, protection, clarity, manifestation, peace, courage, wealth, longevity, wisdom, prosperity, love, renewal, fertility, uplifting, calming, confidence, truth, psychic abilities, spirit work, dreams, past life work, healing, abundance, finances, creativity, manifestation, emotions

Energy   Receptive
Element   Water
Planet   Venus, Neptune
Zodiac   Pisces, Libra, Gemini, Taurus, Aries
Birthstone   March

Kyanite magical properties:
Balance, harmony, calming, connection, psychic abilities, healing, communication, grounding, transformation, meditation, relaxation, luck, growth, leadership, new beginnings, clarity, decisions, stability, truth, vitality, abundance, spirituality, channelling, understanding, dreams

Energy   Receptive
Element   Water
Planet   Jupiter, Venus, Mars
Zodiac   Aries, Libra, Taurus

Labradorite magical properties:
Transformation, cleansing, breaking patterns, potential, psychic abilities, intuition, confidence, spirituality, focus,

protection, imagination, relaxation, soothing, energy, healing, stress, anxiety, luck, abundance, success, decisions, trust, changes, strength, courage, self-confidence, inspiration, perseverance, journeying, clarity, insight, meditation, depression, jealousy, grounding

Energy	Projective
Element	Water
Planet	Earth, Moon, Uranus
Zodiac	Aquarius, Sagittarius, Scorpio, Leo

Lapis lazuli magical properties:
Protection, manifestation, meditation, psychic protection, problem solving, knowledge, clarity, decisions, memory, spirituality, peace, energy, organisation, concentration, stress, luck, negative energy, wealth, abundance, success, love, confidence, truth, renewal, intellect, wisdom, leadership, legal issues, sleep, anxiety, harmony, understanding

Energy	Receptive
Element	Water
Planet	Venus, Jupiter
Zodiac	Sagittarius

Larimar magical properties:
Peace, clarity, healing, inspiration, spirituality, understanding, calming, soothing, uplifting, emotions, fears, depression, patience, creativity, love, communication, friendship, guidance, happiness, decisions, relaxation, meditation, wisdom, divine, harmony

Energy:	Receptive
Element:	Water/Fire/Spirit
Planet:	Neptune
Zodiac:	Pisces

Lepidolite magical properties:
Transformation, soothing, calming, stress, happiness, changes, emotions, psychic abilities, spirituality, depression, divination, connection, strength, uplifting, luck, hope, balance, peace, sleep, harmony, decisions, addiction, releasing, trust, goals, optimism, patience, dreams, opportunities, support, love

Energy	Receptive
Element	Water
Planet	Jupiter, Neptune
Zodiac	Libra

Moonstone magical properties:
New beginnings, moon magic, intuition, calming, psychic abilities, balance, harmony, wishes, cleansing, uplifting, hope, meditation, emotions, love, divination, spirituality, wealth, truth, healing, sensuality, insight, peace, wisdom, communication, confidence, abundance, prosperity, dreams, fertility, travel

Energy	Receptive
Element	Water
Planet	Moon
Zodiac	Cancer, Libra, Scorpio
Birthstone	June, September

Obsidian magical properties:
Truth, healing, clarity, illusions, breaking barriers, integrity, grounding, centring, strength, courage, protection, cleansing, meditation, stress, calming, relaxation, depression, anxiety, wealth, luck, focus, emotions, power, determination, success, patience, perseverance, releasing, spirit work, spirituality, challenges, past life work, divination

Energy	Projective

Element	Fire, Earth, Water
Planet	Saturn, Jupiter
Zodiac	Sagittarius

Pebble/hag stone magical properties:
Protection, fairy magic, nightmares, dreams, healing, fertility, manifestation, negative energy

Energy	Projective
Element	Earth, Water
Planet	Earth

Quartz magical properties:
Purification, cleansing, healing, calming, emotions, strength, support, spirituality, energy, balance, psychic abilities, motivation, uplifting, decisions, anxiety, divine connection, amplifying, focus, meditation, manifestation, channelling, protection, negative energy, clarity, wisdom, concentration, learning, spirit work, communication, astral travel, divination, dreams, harmony

Energy	Projective, Receptive
Planet	Sun, Moon
Element	Fire, Water
Zodiac	Leo, Gemini, Capricorn

Rose quartz magical properties:
Love, happiness, emotions, spirituality, growth, fears, healing, sexuality, passion, calming, soothing, stress, depression, sleep, luck, wisdom, inspiration, success, intuition, grounding, balance, prosperity, self-esteem, harmony, trust, jealousy, gossip, beauty, peace, cleansing, fertility

Energy	Receptive
Element	Earth, Water
Planet	Venus, Moon

Zodiac   Taurus

Selenite magical properties:
Clarity, psychic protection, cleansing, balance, stability, emotions, divine, connections, spirituality, psychic abilities, spirit work, protection, healing, breaking barriers, decisions, intuition, meditation, money, success, love

Energy   Receptive
Element   Water
Planet   Moon
Zodiac   Cancer

Silver magical properties:
Healing, communication, cleansing, energy, intuition, stability, spirituality, patience, perseverance, moon magic, negative energy, protection, balance, psychic abilities, manifestation, wealth, prosperity, abundance, travel, dreams, emotions, purification, love, peace, astral travel

Energy   Receptive
Element   Water
Planet   Moon
Zodiac   Cancer

Sodalite magical properties:
Creativity, communication, peace, friendship, clarity, truth, connection, knowledge, wisdom, emotions, balance, divination, psychic abilities, cleansing, confidence, fears, love, intuition, decisions, perseverance, anxiety, insight, organisation, self-esteem, releasing, understanding, harmony, learning, dreams, meditation

Energy   Receptive
Element   Water
Planet   Jupiter, Venus

Zodiac   Sagittarius

Sugilite magical properties:
Spirituality, wisdom, clarity, insight, courage, truth, passion, inspiration, healing, strength, channelling, psychic abilities, amplification, confidence, focus, love, emotions, releasing, calming, peace, protection, connection, balance, understanding, stress

Energy   Receptive
Element   Water
Planet   Mercury, Jupiter
Zodiac   Virgo

Tourmaline magical properties:
Calming, harmony, balance, insight, spirituality, protection, negative energy, transformation, courage, grounding, fears, creativity, understanding, power, motivation, commitment, patience, stability, releasing, emotions, anxiety, strength, happiness, protection, relaxation, friendship, astral travel

Energy   Receptive (pink, blue, watermelon)
                  Projective (watermelon)
Element   Water (pink, blue, watermelon)
Planet   Venus, Mars
Zodiac   Libra
Birthstone   October

Unakite magical properties:
Love, happiness, growth, wealth, success, harmony, decisions, support, balance, emotions, stability, confidence, strength, anxiety, nature, courage, transformation, releasing, spirituality

Energy   Receptive
Element   Fire, Water
Planet   Mars, Venus, Pluto

Zodiac   Scorpio

Exercise

Keep a record of your crystals and any experiences you have with them. Are there any that you found particularly linked to the element of water?

Water Animals

I love working with animal spirit guides. Each animal has a very unique energy, and they can help and guide you, but also lend their characteristics to your spell work. Each animal has an element that they are associated with, it might be associated with their build, look, habits or where they live. Here are some suggestions for water element animals:

Beaver – Keywords: Creativity, building, teamwork, persistence, appreciation, harmony, doing the best we can, strength, security and good foundations.

Cat – Keywords: Independence, healing, curiosity, mystery, psychic abilities, elegance, intuition, mystery, wisdom, understanding and balance.

Crab – Keywords: Changes, new directions, going with the flow, releasing, security, avoiding obstacles, protection, home life, thinking outside the box, strength, growth, renewal, rebirth, good luck, navigation, different perspective, inner work, meditation.

Crocodile/Alligator – Keywords: Clarity, truth, visions, cycle of life, rebirth, emotions, mysteries and secrets.

Dolphin – Keywords: Wisdom, playfulness, healing, balance, freedom, change, communication, trust, harmony, emotions and water magic.

Dragonfly – Keywords: Magic, mystery, illusion, shape shifting, change, transformation, emotions, compassion, healing, possibilities and enlightenment.

Duck – Keywords: Inner emotions, self-discovery, community, Otherworld communications, prosperity, luck, hope, fidelity, fertility, spirituality, emotions, purification, psychic powers, adaptability, social, friendships, peace, family, be prepared, divination, new opportunities, trust your intuition.

Fish – Keywords: Going beneath the surface, subconscious, emotions, healing, purification, love, relationships, family, cleansing, healing, going with the flow, movement, independence, other realms, motives, awareness, fertility, rebirth, luck, change.

Flamingo – Keywords: Balance, strength, harmony, social, cooperation, liberation, friendship, romance, serenity, contentment, community, trust, destiny.

Frog/Toad – Keywords: Magic, witchcraft, rebirth, new life, awakening, patience, transformation, emotions and intuition.

Hippopotamus – Keywords: Emotions, imagination, intuition, healing, strength, grounding, creativity, inspiration, awareness and perspective.

Lobster – Keywords: Abundance, strength, protection, balance, growth, past life, letting go, releasing negative energy, self-preservation, emotions, psychic abilities, cleansing, self-understanding.

Newt – Keywords: Escape, swiftness, protection, renewal, regeneration, clarity, awareness, fertility, adaptability, releasing the past, sacrifice, transformation.

Octopus – Keywords: Emotions, moon magic, adaptability, spirituality, grounding, letting go, mystery and creativity.

Otter – Keywords: Guidance, psychic abilities, faithfulness, playfulness, exploration, curiosity, recovery, feminine energy, caring, creativity and nurturing.

Pelican – Keywords: Opportunity, patience, observation, self-understanding, emotions, focus, persistence, community, teamwork, progression, movement, parenting, compassion.

Penguin – Keywords: Positive change, adaptability, unconventional, releasing negative energy, social, relationships, community, teamwork, harmony, dreams, intuition, emotions, psychic abilities, portals, balance.

Seagull – Keywords: Emotions, survival, cunning, perseverance, mischievous, selfish, arguments, scavenger, messenger, spirit world. Otherworld, Faerie, communication and behaviour.

Seahorse – Keywords: Partnerships, clarity, perspective, guidance, emotions, navigation, balance, parenting, support, past lives, fidelity, observation, awareness, protection, patience, persistence, grounding.

Seal – Keywords: Transformation, ebb and flow, emotions, imagination, inspiration, intuition, mysteries, balance, harmony, creativity and changes.

Shark – Keywords: Unpredictable, courage, protection, confidence, water magic, visions, psychic work, activity, hunter, survival, adaptability, independence, emotions and balance.

Starfish – Keywords: As above, so below, intuition, duality, balance, spirituality, independence, versatility, non-conformity, renewal, movement, fertility, love, companionship, releasing the past, hope, overcoming challenges, retraining, perseverance.

Swan – Keywords: Beauty, self-esteem, love, the arts, inspiration, inner self, intuition, psychic abilities, going with the flow, acceptance, dedication, commitment and respect.

Turtle – Keywords: Focus, efficiency, direction, steady, pace, acceptance, taking time out, insight, understanding, emotions, peace, strength, determination, overcoming obstacles, serenity.

Walrus – Keywords: Transitions, changes, faith, protection, adaptability, information, intuition, social, wisdom, ancient knowledge, perspective, energy, leadership, guidance, friendship, discovery, dreams.

Whale – Keywords: Wisdom, knowledge, ancestors, rhythms of life, inner voice, spirituality, psychic abilities, creativity, truth and imagination.

Exercise

Keep an eye out for any animals that you see during your day. Not just outside, but also when reading a book, watching TV or adverts in magazines or on billboards. Take note of any animal images you might also see on fabrics, cushions or clothing. If you keep seeing the same one, it may have meaning for you.

Water Animal Meditation

This meditation will help you meet a water animal spirit guide. It may be just a message for you, it might be with you for longer, talk to it and listen.

Find a comfortable place where you won't be disturbed. Take a few deep breaths, in and out...

As your world around you dissipates you find yourself standing at a crossroads, the pathway beneath your feet and heading out in all four directions is a rough dirt track. The sky above you is a dreary grey with the feel of rain on the way.

Looking forwards to the pathway in front of you it looks like it may lead down to the ocean. Turning to your right the pathway there seems as if it may lead down to a fast-running river. Turn again and the pathway behind you looks to lead down to a woodland grove with a pond. And turn again, the pathway to your left appears to lead into a rocky area and you can hear the sound of a waterfall.

Which way will you choose? Trust your intuition.

Heading straight ahead of you, walking along the track, until you find yourself on a sandy beach with the waves from the ocean gently splashing onto the shore. Take a walk along the water's edge. Look carefully at your surroundings, take in all the landscape.

Then find yourself a comfortable place to sit, to look out over the sea. Ask for an animal to make itself known to you. Be patient. If an animal appears, talk to it. Ask questions and listen to the answers. If it doesn't approach you, watch how it moves and take note of what might be a message. Thank the animal. When you are ready walk back along the shore and then to the pathway, back to where you started at the crossroads.

Turning to your right, you walk along the track until you find yourself stepping up onto a small wooden bridge that runs over a fast-moving river. Walk out across the bridge until you reach the centre. Look carefully at your surroundings, take in all the landscape. Turn and look over the side of the bridge and down into the water. Watch the river and it twists and turns and makes its way under the bridge. Ask for an animal to make itself known to you. Be patient. If an animal appears, talk to it. Ask questions and listen to the answers. If it doesn't approach you, watch how it moves and take note of what might be a message. Thank the animal. When you are ready turn and walk back across the bridge and along the track until you reach the centre of the crossroads where you began.

Turning around and heading down the track behind you, walking until you find yourself entering a small grove of trees with lush greenery underneath. In the centre of the grove is a still, dark pond. Make your way to the edge and sit down. Look carefully at your surroundings, take in all the landscape. Ask for an animal to make itself known to you. Be patient. If an animal appears, talk to it. Ask questions and listen to the answers. If it doesn't approach you, watch how it moves and take note of what might be a message. Thank the animal. When you are ready head out of the grove and back along the track to the centre of the crossroads where you began.

Turning to your left and heading down the pathway you find yourself entering a gap between large rocks. As you come out the other side you are faced with a small waterfall, water crashing down from the rocks above into a small clear pool at the base. Sit yourself down beside the base of the waterfall. Look carefully at your surroundings, take in all the landscape. Ask for an animal to make itself known to you. Be patient. If an animal appears, talk to it. Ask questions and listen to the answers. If it doesn't approach you, watch how it moves and take note of what might be a message. Thank the animal. Turn and make your way back out through the rocks and along the pathway to the centre of the crossroads where you began.

Know that you can come back to the crossroads at any time and travel down any of the pathways.

When you are ready, slowly and gently come back to the here and now.

Exercise

Write down your water animal experience, if you met a particular animal do some research on it.

Water Deities

Each deity is usually associated with one of the elements more than the others. Please do your research first. I would never recommend calling upon a god without knowing a proper amount of information about them first. Learn about their culture, myths and stories before you ask for their help. Here are some suggestions for deities that correspond with the element of water, the list is only a start, there are a lot more. I have only given brief descriptions, if any of them sing out to you, I encourage you to research and investigate further.

Amphitrite – Ancient Greek goddess/queen of the sea, she is wife to Poseidon and eldest of the Nereides. She is the female personification of the sea and mother to dolphins, seals and all the fish in the sea. Depicted as a young woman, sometimes holding a fish or riding in a chariot drawn by fish tailed horses. Call upon her for strength, transformation, power of the sea.

Anuket – Egyptian goddess of the crescent Moon. She is responsible for the annual flooding of the river Nile. She watches over agriculture and all food growth along with wealth and prosperity. Call upon her for: Wealth, prosperity, growth, fertility, nourishment, contentment.

Aphrodite – Greek Goddess of love and war and Goddess of sexual passion, love, pleasure and physical beauty. Her name derives from the Greek word for 'foam' as she was believed to have been born from the white foam produced by the severed genitals (eek!) of Uranus after his son threw them in the sea. She rules marriages and the love that holds them together but is also the Goddess of illicit affairs. She teaches about dedication and self-love, but she is also known to have a quick and occasionally unscrupulous response to any requests. Work with her for passion, love, pleasure, beauty, self-love and marriages.

Arianrhod – Welsh goddess of the Moon. She forms the triple goddess triad with Blodeuwedd and Cerridwen. Her name translates as 'silver disc', she is often referred to as Goddess of the Silver Wheel. Arianrhod guides the dead to the other side and rules the sky and the sea as well as the Moon. She can shapeshift into an owl. She is also known as one of the goddesses of Avalon. Call upon her for: Moon magic, dream work, psychic abilities, divination, past lives, reincarnation, other realms, feminine power, retribution, karma.

Coventina – Goddess of natural springs, fresh waters that flow through the landscape – the mountains, grassy hills and riverbanks, the deepest caves and well. Coventina is a water nymph or water spirit, and she is depicted as being a Mother Goddess, wearing flowing robes which merge with the waters that she is, carrying a water vessel in one hand and a water lily in the other. She was most prominent in Northumberland, England – particularly near the famous Hadrian's Wall, where a temple dedicated to her was found, although she was also worshipped in Northwest Spain and Southern France. Call upon her for inspiration, purification, childbirth, renewal, abundance, wishes and prosperity.

Fontus – Roman god of wells and springs and all flowing waters. Believed to be the son of the god Janus. Call upon him for new beginnings, wishes, emotions and going with the flow.

Hapi – Ancient Egyptian god who is the personification of the annual flooding of the river Nile. He was patron of upper and lower Egypt. Often depicted as twin deities Hap-Reset (upper) and Hap-Meht (lower) pouring water from a jug or tying together papyrus and lotus plants. Work with him for fertility and bringing together.

Hekate – Greek goddess of the dark Moon. She covers new beginnings and magic of all kinds. She walks the ancient roads and pathways, particularly associated with crossroads, those where three roads cross. She forms a triad with Persephone and Demeter, she being the Crone aspect. She guards the spirit world and wields power over all realms. She is one seriously intimidating goddess, but wise beyond words. Call upon her for: Moon magic, witchcraft, herb magic, necromancy, protection, prosperity, new beginnings, decisions, mysteries, knowledge, learning, inner work, shadow work.

Inanna – Sumerian goddess of the full Moon and the stars, also known as Ishtar in Babylon. She is Queen of heaven and earth. She has a reputation for being a little bit saucy which led her to be linked to fertility rituals. She does look after her followers, dishing out the rules and keeping them safe. Call upon her for: Love, fertility, warrior, strength, courage, seduction, sensuality, protection, justice.

Isis – Egyptian goddess Queen of Egypt. She is looked upon as Mother Moon, Queen of Sorcery, and the life force within the river Nile. Isis taught her people useful skills, those they would need to survive and flourish, no being high up in the sky for this one, she got down with her subjects (very practical woman). Call upon her for: Magic, dreams, divination, harvest, perspective, love, spirituality, faithfulness, destiny, revitalisation, fulfilment, inner beauty, spirituality, rebirth, feminine energy, knowledge, motherhood, healing, changes, manifesting.

Manannán mac Lir – An Irish sea god who had a number of magical items such as impenetrable armour, an invincible sword and a chariot the rides across the waves of the sea. He provides abundance in the form of crops and gives protection to all those who sail the seas. He is part of the Tuatha De Danann race. His title is Lord of the Sea, and he was also known to be a master of illusions. Call upon him for weather magic, guidance, protection for sea travel, abundance and Otherworld connections.

Nehalennia – Goddess of the North Sea, either Germanic or Celtic. Depicted on a throne holding a basket of apples or bread she is often seen with a wolfy type dog beside her. Other images show her standing beside a ship. Offerings are made to her for safe passage across the North Sea. Call upon her for safe travel over the North Sea! Also for peace and prosperity.

Nephthys – Egyptian goddess of the dark Moon, the dead, darkness, and the shadows. She is the dark to the light of Isis. Call upon her for: Death and rebirth, night magic, protection, shadow work, grief, spirit work, devotion, reincarnation, power, magic.

Neptune – Originally a Roman god of fresh water he later became a god of the sea, equated with the Greek god Poseidon. He also controls the winds and storms. He carries a trident and rides in a chariot across the sea pulled by horses or sea creatures. Call upon him for weather magic, dreams, the arts, clarity, mysteries, intuition, sacrifice.

Nereides – from ancient Greek mythology, the Nereids/Nereides are fifty sea nymphs, all daughters of Nereus, the old man of the sea. Goddesses to all that the sea can provide and bringing in protection for sailors and fishermen. Call upon the Nereides for protection in sea travel, abundance and skills of the sea.

Njord – Norse god of the sea, the wind and all that the ocean offers. He was often called upon originally to help with sea travel and hunting. If you are worthy, he also bestows you with wealth and prosperity. Call upon him for travel, weather magic, hunting, wealth and prosperity.

Oceanus – A Greek Titan god who rules the river Okeanos that provides fresh water to all the rivers, wells and springs along with making it rain. The heavenly bodies were believed to have risen from his waters. Depicted as a bull horned god with the tail of a serpent like fish. Call upon him for weather magic, divine connection, strength, fertility.

Olokun – Olokun is a Yoruba Orisha ruling over the seas. There are many different tales about him, some say he is male with a number of wives, others seem to believe he was a she. Some stories accuse him of a quick temper, so much so that he attempted to send a flood to wipe out all humans because they annoyed him (I feel for him). Call upon him for sea magic, strength and he would probably work well for cursing too.

Oshun – Oshun is the African Yoruba Orisha of water. She is always represented as a beautiful woman and in some cultures, she is said to be a mermaid. Whenever Oshun is encountered it is said she is always dancing. One of the main stories of hers speaks of her broken heart. And so, she forever dances and sings to soothe her heartache. But she is not a goddess to be messed with. Her temper is something rarely seen but when trifled with her calming dancing ceases and the tsunamis and tidal waves begin. But other than this she is loved by all and well known for her healing of the sick. She believes very much in diplomacy and fighting is not her forte. She was taught by the primordial deities the use of divination using cowrie shells. And she passed the knowledge onto us humans making her the goddess of prophecy. Call upon her for love, romance, passion, divination, healing, diplomacy, order, prophecy, dance and fertility.

Poseidon – Ancient Greek Olympian god covering the sea, floods, drought, earthquakes and horses. He carries a trident and rides across the waves in a chariot pulled by horse type sea creatures called hippocamps. He sometimes carries a boulder encrusted with sea creatures. He does not have a good disposition, said to be moody, greedy and bad tempered. Call upon him for, well I am not sure you would want to really, but I bet he casts a good curse. He would, however, be useful for bravery and strength.

Sabrina – Sabrina is a goddess of the River Severn, which begins its journey in Wales, flowing through Shropshire, Worcestershire and Gloucestershire in England and ending up in the sea. Call upon her for protection, boundaries, wishes, blessings, emotions, movement, going with the flow, freedom and self-worth.

Selene – From ancient Greece, she is a Titan Moon goddess, sister of Helios (the Sun). She drives a silver chariot drawn by two white horses, across the sky each night. The Roman equivalent is Luna. Call upon her for: Moon magic, dream work, sleep, Moon phases, magic, divination, sensuality.

Sulis – The ancient hot springs in Bath, Somerset, England are the home of the English goddess Sulis – her name meaning 'eye' or 'gap' in reference to the spring from which her waters flowed and her powers as seeress. Her name also meant 'sun' as she was often looked upon as a Solar Deity. The Romans called her Sulis Minerva – an amalgamation of Sul, Goddess of healing and their own deity Minerva, a Goddess of Wisdom. The waters were used for healing, regeneration and fertility. Women would come for help in childbearing and lactation issues. They would immerse in the baths, drink the waters or sleep in the shrine hoping the Goddess Sulis would hear their pleas. Call upon her for healing, fertility, finding lost objects, justice, confidence, success, pride.

Tefnut – Ancient Egyptian goddess of moisture and rainfall. Her twin was the god of air. Depicted with the head of a lioness she often wore a solar disc and cobra symbols. Her name may translate as 'one who spits'. She brings balance in the form of water and sun. It is believed she represents the transformation of tears into vengeance. Call upon her for balance, vengeance, transformation.

Yemaya – An Orisha, an African goddess of water. Yemaya is honoured as the mother of the sea and the moon. She is the keeper of the female mysteries and a guardian of women. She aids in the conception of children and their births, protecting and blessing infants until they hit puberty. She is a healing goddess, showing compassion and kindness to those in need. Yemaya is the personification of rivers and bodies of water and is sometimes depicted as a mermaid. Call upon her for feminine energy, protection, childbirth, children, healing, compassion, kindness.

Water Deity Meditation
Find a comfortable place where you won't be disturbed. Take a few deep breaths, in and out...

As your world around you dissipates you find yourself standing outside a large stone temple with columns flanking the entrance. The sky above you is grey, and it is just starting to rain. You head through the temple entrance to escape the rain. Once inside you take a look around. It is a large open space, each wall covered with beautiful and colourful mosaics. Walk around and take in the images. In the centre of the room stands a huge ornate foundation, carved with dolphins and sirens. You head towards the fountain and sit on the edge. Trail your hand into the water, it is cool and refreshing.

As you sit quietly listening to the sound of the fountain, water splashing gently onto the surface and trailing your hand in the cool waters you hear a sound. Someone enters the room. You look up to see a figure carrying a large jug and heading towards you. What do they look like?

They sit themselves down beside you and dip the jug into the water from the fountain and set it safely on the floor. They reach out and take hold of both your hands, looking into your eyes. They ask if you have any questions, anything that the power of water can help you with. You answer them. Talk for as long as you need to and listen to their advice.

When you are finished, they release your hands and pick up the jug. You thank them for their council, and they turn and head back the way they came.

Sit for a few moments thinking about your conversation. Then make your way back out of the temple to where you began.

Slowly and gently come back to the here and now.

Exercise

Do some research about the deity you met in your meditation. Find out the myths and stories. If you want to work with them further, you could even set up an altar dedicated to them.

Water Rituals

We probably all have our own way of working rituals. I have given my suggestion here but go with what works for you. I have included quarter calls for all four elements because I like the balance and I think the elements support each other. However, you could just call upon the element of water if you prefer.

I have given a ritual template here, use the deity list within this book for your gods and goddesses and also spell work to include, or add your own. I suggest you work a ritual for only one intent at a time, don't mix them up, it could confuse the energy.

Calling the Quarters

When in ritual most pagans will 'call in the quarters'. What does that mean? Well, we invite the four elements to join us and add their energy and qualities to the ritual. Each element corresponding to the four compass points. Some traditions choose to call in the Watchtowers or Guardians of the Watchtowers. The Guardians refer to the raw elementals and the Watchtowers are the directions.

Circle Casting

Cast a circle to keep the positive energy raised within and to protect you from any negative outside influences. If you have the space, you can walk the circle clockwise (to bring in energy) and perhaps sprinkle soil, salt or a corresponding water herb or flower if you wish. If your space is limited, you can turn on the spot and visualise the circle. Make sure you 'see' the circle. Not only go around you but also above and below. You should end up with a visualised sphere or bubble around you. As you cast the circle you might like to add a chant such as:

I cast this circle round about
To keep unwanted energy out
Bringing in the element of water flow
I cast this circle, my magic now to go
Make it so!

Being a bit of a Star Trek fan, I tend to use the phrase 'make it so' rather than 'so mote it be'. You may prefer to use your own words.

Call in Your Quarters

Your options are to just turn and face each direction as you call them in. Or you might like to light a candle at each direction. You could use items such as lighting incense in the east, a candle in the south, a dish of water in the west and a dish of soil in the north. If space is lacking you could work with a shell for west, a pebble for earth, a feather for air and a match for south. As we are working with the element of water specifically you may just want to place a candle in the west and no items at all at the other points.

I start my quarter calls in the north, it seems to be the obvious compass point choice to me. A lot of witches and pagans start in the north. Although druids tend to begin their rituals by saluting the sun as it rises in the east. From the start point I turn clockwise. Give a call for each quarter, something like:

"Element of earth
I invite you this ritual to tend

From the direction of North
Stability and grounding your energy to lend
Hail and welcome!

Element of air
I invite you this ritual to tend
From the direction of East
Intellect and wisdom your energy to lend
Hail and welcome!

Element of fire
I invite you this ritual to tend
From the direction of South
Passion and power your energy to lend
Hail and welcome!

Element of water
I invite you this ritual to tend
From the direction of West
Emotions and intuition your energy to lend
Hail and welcome!"

Deity

It is entirely up to you whether you call upon deity or not. If you do, please make sure you do your research first. Not only would it be impolite to call upon a god that you don't know anything about, but it could also lend entirely the wrong energy to your ritual. Think about working a ritual for love and calling upon a war god...messy doesn't even begin to describe it.

Obviously, this book is all about the element of water so I have suggested a list of water deities, but you may be drawn in another direction. Trust your intuition but definitely do your homework too. I usually call upon a god and a goddess when working ritual, for me it brings a balance. But you don't have to, if you prefer to just call a god or a goddess then go for it. You may just prefer to call upon Mother Earth instead. Call in your deity with something like this:

"I call upon the goddess Coventina,
Asking that you bring your gifts of inspiration, abundance and
prosperity to me
Hail and welcome"

Basically, you call them by name and then ask them to bring whatever energy you need, so for Coventina you would ask her to bring the positive energy of abundance and inspiration.

If you were performing a ritual with the intent of uncovering secrets, you might call upon Neptune with:

"I call upon the god Neptune,
Asking that you show me the hidden truths and provide clarity of
sight
Hail and welcome"

If it is healing you are after, then Yemaya would be your gal:

"I call upon the goddess Yemaya
Asking that you bring me the gift of healing and compassion
Hail and welcome"

Spell Work
Any ritual is created with a purpose, an intent in mind. What do you want to work this ritual for? Whatever it might be, this is the point in the ritual when you work your spell or even just use a meditation. Check out the spells and meditations suggested within this book or work with your own.

To the Feast and Drink!

Once your spell work or meditation is done it is time for the feast! This really has double purpose. One is to celebrate with food and drink. A bit of a blessing in the form of 'may you never thirst' and 'may you never hunger'. Some of the food and drink is often sprinkled onto the earth if you are outside as a thank you to the gods and nature. Feasting also helps you to ground during the ritual, after any energy work has been done. It doesn't matter what you use to eat and drink. At our Kitchen Witch rituals, we always have cake, because that's how we roll. Often, I make cake that corresponds to the intent of the ritual, using particular ingredients and flavours to add to the will of the event. But you can use bread, sweets, fruits or biscuits. Mead or wine is a traditional ritual drink, but anything goes. At our rituals we often theme it, so we might have flavoured waters or herbals teas and in the cold, we have even had hot chocolate.

Now you close it all down in reverse...

Deity

Don't forget your manners, deity need to be thanked for attending the proceedings. It doesn't need to be fancy, just a simple one or two lines.

> *"I thank the god/goddess for lending your energy to the rite today. Hail and furewell"*

It really is that easy. But of course, you can add more text if you prefer.

Quarters

Next is thanking the elements in turn for their energy. Work in reverse order to that which you used initially. I start in the

North when inviting the elements in, so I would now start with thanking water and working backwords to earth (North).

Again, it doesn't need to be fancy, just something along the lines of:

"I thank the element of earth for being here today, hail and farewell"

But I have made longer suggestions below:

"Element of water
From the direction of West
Thank you for the energy you lent
Hail and farewell!

Element of fire
From the direction of South
Thank you for the energy you lent
Hail and farewell!

Element of air
From the direction of East
Thank you for the energy you lent
Hail and farewell!

Element of earth
From the direction of North
Thank you for the energy you lent
Hail and farewell!"

Circle
Now the circle must be uncast. Walk widdershins (anti clockwise) around the circle and visualise the globe that you created, dispersing into the wind or back down into the soil.

"I uncast this circle now the magic is all done
With my thanks for protection it gave
This circle is now open, but never broken
So mote it be!"

Don't forget to give an offering to the earth if you didn't do so during the feasting. Dispose of any leftover spell working items and/or candles. Always leave the area clean and free from litter once you depart.

Water Spells

The element of water aligns itself to several different intents, here are some of my suggestions for water related spells. Follow them as I have laid them out or use them as a starting point to adjust with your own personal tweaks.

Dream Witch Bottle

Witch bottles can be used for all sorts of different intents, but they do work well as a dream tool. Create your witch bottle and place it beside your bed to help increase your prophetic dreams. Go with your intuition about what to add, but here are the ingredients I use.

You will need:

A small clean jar or bottle with a cork or lid
A piece of cobweb from your home to represent you and your web of life
A blend of herbs that all correspond with dream work such as ash keys, chamomile, eucalyptus, heather and jasmine
A blend of herbs to enhance your psychic abilities such as marigold, mugwort, rose and star anise

A crystal chip or small tumble stone that helps with dream work such as agate, green aventurine or quartz
Candle for dripping wax, I like lilac or white for dream bottles
Matches or lighter

Charge each of your ingredients individually as you add them to the bottle.

You might like to say a chant as you do so, something like:

"A witch bottle for dreaming and insight
Magic of the ingredients help me at night
Prophetic dreams and guidance as I sleep
May this magic take my dreams in deep"

When you have added all that you want, put the cork in the bottle or put the lid on. I like to now light a candle and hold it over the lid/cork so that the wax drips on and over to seal it. Once the bottle is complete you can hold it in both hands and charge it with your intent once again.

Protection Floor Wash

You can create floor wash for any kind of intent, but within the home I like to bring in the magical elements of cleansing and protection when I do the housework.

You will need:

A bucket or large bowl
Hot water
Dash of washing up liquid (or your usual cleaning fluid)
A few drops of ginger essential oil for cleansing and protection
A few drops of peppermint essential oil for cleansing and protection

Fill the bucket with hot water, add your cleaning fluid and the essential oil. Give it a stir and it is ready to use. You might like to say a chant as you are stirring, something like:

"Mint and ginger hot and mean
Help me get this household clean
Herbal powers to bring protection in"

Use the water to clean your floors, window sills and any area that will take a bit of water.

Freezer Spell

If you find yourself in the situation where someone is causing you grief, you can bind them with a freezer spell. It won't cause them actual physical harm, but it should help stop them from bothering you.

You will need:

A small plastic container that will go in the freezer
A slip of paper
A pen
A few black pepper corns
Pinch of chilli flakes
Black food colouring
Water

Take the slip of paper and write the name of the person you need to leave you alone on it. This can also work with bad habits you want to get rid of, write the habit on the slip of paper. Put the paper in the base of the plastic container. Put a few black peppercorns on top of the paper along with a pinch of chilli flakes.

Now pour water over the top until it covers the paper and herbs, they will float, just give them a prod to soak them. Now add a few drops of black food colouring and give the water a swirl. Hold the container in your hands and say:

"Water black, peppercorns too
Chilli flakes from me to you
Bring protection in for me
Make me invisible for you to see"

Pop the lid on and carefully place the container in the freezer. It can stay there until the situation has resolved.

Healing Candle Spell

Healing magic can be greatly enhanced with the magical energy of water.

You will need:

Spell candle, I like to use blue to correspond with healing
Candle holder
Matches or a lighter
Dish of water, big enough to lay the candle in on its side
Sea salt
Knife or pin
Dried thyme leaves

Take a big pinch of sea salt and sprinkle it into the dish of water, saying:

"Healing salt from the sea, bring your magic and make it be"

Take the candle and carve the name or initials of the person who needs healing into the side of it. Now roll the candle in the salt water until it is covered. Take the candle out of the water and sprinkle or roll it in the dried thyme leaves saying:

"Magic leaf of thyme, healing energy be mine"

Set the candle in the holder and light the wick. Now focus on the flame and visualise the poorly person becoming well again. Allow the candle to burn out completely. Any left-over water or herbs can be sprinkled outside on the soil.

Ritual Bath Bombs

These are fairly easy to make and can be tailored to suit your intent by using corresponding herbs and plant matter. I have given the basic recipe here and an idea for a releasing recipe.

Basic recipe:

400g/14 oz sodium bicarbonate
200g/7 oz citric acid
2 - 3 teaspoons dried flower petals
1 teaspoon vegetable oil or cocoa butter
15 drops essential oil
1 teaspoon water

This recipe makes 20 bath bombs which will keep for up to three months. Lightly grease an ice cube or pop cake mould. Measure out all the dry ingredients and give them a mix together. Melt the cocoa butter in a glass bowl over a pan of warm water and add the essential oils. Pour the melted mixture into the dry ingredients and mix to combine. Add the teaspoon of water sprinkling it over the mixture. Give it all a mix until it feels and looks like damp sand and sticks together. If it is too crumbly add a bit more water, but only a tiny amount at a time. Press the mixture into the mould firmly and allow to set, it will take at least an hour. Turn out of the moulds and store in a cool, dry place.

For releasing bath bombs add:

1 teaspoon dried carnation petals
1 teaspoon dried thyme leaves
8 drops geranium essential oil
7 drops mint essential oil

Seven Shell Spell

Try saying that fast! This brings the power of the ocean into your spell working using shells that nature provides and some sea water. This spell can be used for many different types of intent whether it is bringing something to you, prosperity, healing, moving an issue along or any other type of reason. You just need to tailor it to suit. I work with the number seven, over seven days but be guided by your intuition.

You will need:

Seven shells
A small amount of sea water (or water with salt added)

Lay each of your shells out in a line on your altar, turn them so that the outer side of the shell is faced upwards.

On the first day turn the first shell over and dab some salt water inside it.
Make your request, so you might say *"with my shell number one, I request *insert intent here* has begun"*
On day two turn the second shell over and dab some salt water inside it.

Make your request, so you might say *"with my shell number two, I request *insert intent here* makes it through"*
On day three turn over the third shell and dab some salt water inside it.
Make your request, so you might say *"with my shell number three, I request *insert intent here* I now see"*
On day four turn over the fourth shell and dab some salt water inside it.
Make your request, so you might say *"with my shell number four, I request *insert intent here* is no more/sends me more"*
On day five turn over the fifth shell and dab with salt water inside.
Make your request, so you might say *"with my shell number five, I request *insert intent here* keeping this magic alive"*
On day six turn over the sixth shell and dab inside with salt water.
Make your request, so you might say *"with my shell number six, I request *insert intent here* goes into the mix"*
On day seven turn over the seventh shell and dab the inside with salt water.
Make your request, so you might say *"with my shell number seven, my spell work is done"*

You can leave the shells on your altar until the spell comes to fruition or you can offer them back to the sea.

Motivation Spell
If you need a spell to help get a project or situation moving, then water is a perfect medium to work with. I like to work with this spell over seven days to build momentum and power, but you could work with six days, nine or whatever number you feel is right.

You will need:

> *A small dish*
> *Blessed/moon/spring water*
> *Cinnamon (ground or essential oil)*
> *Ginger (ground or essential oil)*

On the first day place the bowl in the centre of your altar. Add a splash of blessed water, and a pinch or few drops each of cinnamon and ginger.

This is an offering with a request to help whatever it is to move forward. I work with Sulis, so I make my offerings to her, but go with a deity you like to work with or just ask help from the element of water. Say something along the lines of:

> *"Water fast and flowing strong,*
> *Help my situation/venture move along*
> *A kick of spice to make it go fast*
> *Bring things along at long last"*

Repeat your offering into the same bowl every day for seven days. Any remnants in the bowl can then be offered to the earth.

Water Releasing Spell

This spell works for anything you wish to release, cleanse or get rid of and uses the power of water to do so.

You will need:

> *A slip of paper*
> *Water soluble ink or paint*
> *A shallow dish*
> *Water*

Write that which you wish to release on the slip of paper. It might be one word, a person's name or a bad habit. Place the slip of paper in the base of the dish. Pour water over the top until the dish is half full. You can say something like:

"Water cleansing, pure and clean
Dissolve, dispel and make it unseen"

Leave the water to dissolve the words from the paper. Once that is done it can be tipped onto the earth. If it is raining outside this is an ideal spell to utilise the weather. Write your words on the paper and pop it outside, secure it with pebbles and allow the rain to wash away the words.

Tree Blessing

Most of us will have a tree at Yule or maybe even Samhain, all decked out with lights and sparkles. Before you decorate your tree how about giving it a blessing to bring abundance, prosperity and positive energy in? It doesn't matter if it is a real or fake one, the blessing works just the same. If you have green garlands and wreaths for decoration these can be blessed to.

You will need:

A dish of water
Salt
Incense or a scented candle
Lighter or matches

Work this magic once your tree is set in place but before you decorate it. Light your incense or scented candle. Take your dish of water and add a pinch of salt, stir it with your finger clockwise. Stand in front of your tree and walk around it clockwise. three times. As you walk dip your fingers into the salt water and flick it onto the tree. (Just lightly, you don't want to soak the tree!).

On the first circle say:
"I give blessings to this tree, that it may be a sign of great positivity"
On the second circle say:
"Water is my blessing to thee, to bring abundance and prosperity"
On the third circle say:
"Salt of earth and power of life, to keep away stress and strife"

Now stand in front of the tree and say:

"Blessings to my festive tree
To bring abundance and prosperity
With love and light and power to me
My thanks and gratitude to thee"

Simmering Pot

This spell is very useful if you cannot work with incense smoke. It works with the magic of water but also has the added bonus of making the house smell delightful. It can be tailored for any intent.

You will need:

A saucepan
Water
Wooden spoon

Spices of your choice, I have given my recipe here for success and prosperity:

One cinnamon stick or a heaped teaspoon of ground cinnamon
A piece of root ginger or a heaped teaspoon of ground ginger

An orange, sliced
A teaspoon of ground nutmeg
Three star anise

Fill your saucepan half full with water. Break the cinnamon stick in half and pop it in the water or add the ground cinnamon. Stir the pan three times in a clockwise direction and say:

"Cinnamon spice and all things nice
Now I stir the water around thrice
Bring success and money my way
Money and success come this day"

Next take the root ginger and slice it or use ground ginger, add it to the pan. Stir the pan three times in a clockwise direction and say:

"Ginger spice and all things nice
Now I stir the water around thrice
Success and prosperity come my way
Bring these things now within this day"

Add the slices of orange to the pan. Stir the water three times in a clockwise direction and say:

"Orange slices and all things nice
Now I stir the water around thrice
Generosity may come my way
I will also give generosity this day"

Add the ground nutmeg to the pan. Stir the water three times in a clockwise direction and say:

"Nutmeg spice and all things nice

Now I stir the water around thrice
Luck and money will come my way
Bring prosperity to me this day"

Now heat the pan on a low temperature. It needs to simmer until the scent of the ingredients fill the air throughout your home. You can keep it on a very low heat for an hour or two to really get the full affect. Once you are done, put the ingredients into your compost bin or trash and pour the water onto the soil in your garden if possible.

Suggestions

Healing – for a healing simmering pot try using:
An apple, sliced
Three bay leaves
A piece of root ginger sliced or a teaspoon of ground ginger
A heaped teaspoon of dried thyme leaves

Cleansing and Purifying – for a simmering pot to clear negative energy try using:
A heaped teaspoon of dried mint leaves
Three bay leaves
A teaspoon of fennel seeds
A teaspoon of lavender flowers
A lemon, sliced

Floating Candle Love Spell

The element of water very much covers love spells as it is all about emotions. But I do have a warning with using love spells. Often people think the solution to a relationship situation is to just throw a spell at it. Relationships are hard work; they take time and effort and if you don't put that into it then things go wrong. Things can go wrong in relationships anyway, that's life. Do the work...see what you can do to resolve the issues but sometimes it just happens and there isn't a thing you can do about it but deal with the situation as best you can and move on with your life.

The other scenario is using a love spell to attract a soul mate, often this is for someone specific, and I must say...this can only end badly. We are involving free will here...Do you really want to cast a spell and have the man/woman of your desire go out with you purely on the strength of a spell? Wouldn't you rather know that someone was with you because they truly liked you? Love spells are useful for drawing a soul mate if you aren't particularly targeting a specific person, in fact they work very well if you want to spice up your current love life or keep fidelity in your relationship. When you want to write that love spell to attract someone to you, I would recommend you really leave it loosely worded and up to the universe, it usually knows best because what we want isn't always what we need. And of course, love spells can also be about self-love – and we all need to do that!

You will need:

A floating candle or a small tealight
Lighter or matches
A shallow dish
Water
Rose petals

Place the dish on a flat safe surface, your altar would be good if it fits. Fill the dish about three quarters full with water. Now carefully float the candle on the surface of the water. Take a few rose petals and scatter them on the water and then light the candle. Sit quietly for a few moments watching the candle flame. Now speak your request, you can just say words from the heart or a little chant. Here is my suggestion:

"Universe of great power
Drawing upon water magic at this hour
Light my way through emotions clear
And bring my perfect soul mate near"

If you are working with self-love, you could adjust the words to:

"Universe of great power
Drawing upon water magic at this hour
Light my way through emotions near
And show me self-care and love so clear"

Once the candle has burn out the water and petals can be offered to the earth.

Shells

Living near the sea I am lucky enough to be able to collect seashells easily, I love walking along the beach and always come back with pockets full of shells and hag stones. So how about the magical properties of the humble seashell? Obviously, seashells are associated with water, I often use a shell to represent west when I am in ritual, I also use them in water element witch bottles. The Moon controls the tides of the ocean, so shells are also associated with the lunar magic. Being associated with water and the Moon I think the shell works perfectly in spells for emotions too. Shells also have an association with the goddess Aphrodite, so can also be used for love spells. Use a shell as a love drawing talisman.

In the past shells were also used in some parts of the world as currency so they also have the association of money and prosperity. Use in money drawing medicine bags (with a silver coin and some mint or basil) or pop a small shell in your purse.

Think about what a shell is, it is a protective covering for the creature inside making shells also good for protection. Use them in your witch bottles or strung on a necklace for this purpose. You can also pop a shell on the collar of your dog or cat to bring protection.

Shells can also be used in divination, use in a set with pebbles, crystals and bones to cast a reading. Shells can also have runes or symbols carved or painted on them. Particular shells also have their own individual meanings:

Abalone – General use and containment of empowered herbs and stones. Also very good for love spells, balance and affirmations. An abalone amulet will protect against negative energy. Abalone talismans will bring creativity. Wearing an abalone shell will bring protection against negative energy but also protection from depression, sorrow and fear. The abalone shell also brings creativity and inspiration. Abalone make good tools to use for balancing your chakras because it carries the colours of the rainbow. Abalone shells also make good holders for incense.

Auger – (And any long pointy shaped shells) due to their shape they bring a masculine energy...and can be used for fertility, strength, protection or courage.

Clam shells – Purification and love but also friendships.

Conch shell – This shell is used to make a loud noise when blown so it works well for summoning spells, communication and clearing away confusion. It is also a symbol of truthful speech and strength and love.

Cockles – Love, friendship, relationships and emotions.

Cone shells – Time to take charge and lead by example with this shell but it may also indicate a situation where you need to retreat or take cover.

Cowrie shell – Prosperity, money, love and fertility – if you look at a cowrie shell it looks very 'feminine' (i.e., yoni shaped). String cowrie shells onto red cord or a thread long enough to hang over your tummy for fertility and once you are pregnant to protect your unborn child. Make a necklace from charged cowrie shells to wear for general protection.

Whelks – Dramatic positive change and getting a grip on a situation. Also, useful for decision and direction spell work.

Limpets – Courage, confidence, endurance and strength.

Scallops – A good all-purpose shell but also for travel and movement.

Oysters – Good fortune, love and passion but also for banishing spell work.

Sand dollars (echinoids) – Wisdom and knowledge.

Moon snails – Lunar magic, psychic abilities, purification and peace.

If you are collecting your own seashells, please make sure that the creature is not still inside it, if you do pick up one with a living creature toss it back into the water. If you are purchasing your seashells in a shop or from the internet, please make sure they are from sustainable and viable sources.

If you collected the shells from the seashore then I don't think they need any preparation, they have the energy of the sea and the sun already in them. If, however, you purchased your shells from a store you might like to sit them in a bowl of salt water for a few hours, in the sunlight if you can.

Exercise

Keep a record of any shells you find; try to identify what they are and note how well they worked in any magic that you use them for.

Driftwood

Along a lot of seashores you can find driftwood, although it does seem to depend on the particular shore and area. Driftwood carries the energy of earth from the tree it once was and also the magic of the sea and the element of water, so it gives a double whammy.

What you do with your pieces of driftwood depends on what shape and size they are, but you could string them into a wind chime, drill out holes to use as a tea light holder, craft into a wand or use as a small altar. If you have enough small pieces, you could also make a divination set. Or create a mixed set using shells, sea pebbles and driftwood.

When you collect any driftwood check it first for animal or plant life because it is often used as shelter by small animals and birds.

In Norse mythology the god Odin and his brothers Vili and Ve created the first humans Ask and Embla from two pieces of driftwood, one was ash and the other elm. Vikings apparently also had the habit of throwing pieces of wood into the sea before they landed on the shore, where the wood ended up was the site for their main hall to be built and the piece of wood used to create a high seat inside.

Sea Glass

Sea glass isn't found on the beach near me, but I am lucky enough to have family that live on the Jurassic Coast here in the UK where the beaches are littered with sea glass. What is it? Well it is actually nature's way of recycling broken bottles and jars that find their way into the ocean. The pieces of glass are tumbled smooth by the natural motion of the waves. Apparently, it takes about ten years for a piece of broken glass to become proper sea glass i.e. a small piece of smooth frosted looking glass pebble.

For me, sea glass can be used in magic just as seashells would, it is directly connected with the element of water and holds all the emotional properties that water brings but as it was originally glass it also has a fiery element to it as well. Use in any kind of magical workings but it can also be made into pretty talismans or jewellery.

Colour Magic

I love to work with colour magic. It brings its own energy to spells and rituals. Bringing in a colour to represent an element can help not only boost your magic but help you to connect with that element. Water is often represented by the colour blue. This makes sense to me. However, go with what works for you. I have listed below my idea for water colours.

Blue – water magic, healing, peace, balance, calm, tranquillity, understanding, emotions, sleep, reassurance, spirituality, inspiration, wisdom, loyalty, purification, protection, hope, psychic work, health, dreams, astral travel, meditation, communication, creativity, truth, patience, harmony, friendship

Grey – stability, decisions, binding, compromise, intellect, negotiations, elegance, mysteries, reason, wisdom

White – peace, conscious, moon magic, feminine energy, purity, truth, psychic abilities, spirit work, spirituality, enlightenment, spiritual strength, aura work, healing, cleansing, defence, The Goddess, astral travel, innocence, meditation, divination, consecration

Green – earth magic, fertility, success, prosperity, money, luck, growth, healing, rejuvenation, plant and tree magic, employment, abundance, energy, balance, generosity, goals, ambition, marriage, nature spirits, harmony, optimism, fairy magic, working against greed and jealousy

Black – protection, hexing, sobriety, absorbing, wisdom, changes, rebirth, meditation, removing bad habits, banishing, mourning, depression, illness, control, discipline, dispelling negativity, reversing, uncrossing/unhexing, binding, spirit work, defence, repelling, confusion, shape shifting, The Crone

Water Divination
Water provides a natural scrying and divination tool. You can set it up with a scrying bowl or use what Mother Nature provides and read messages or symbols in puddles or ponds.

Hydromancy
Hydromancy is divination using the medium of water. It covers all forms of reading images and symbols in the reflective surface that water provides. Throw a pebble into a pool of water and what do you get? Ripples...and by watching and translating the ripples, the ebb and the flow of the water you can get your answers.

Water Scrying

I like to use a bowl that has a dark inside and fill it with water then I add something to help the images such as popping a silver coin in the bottom, or you could scatter flower petals, leaves or herbs onto the surface. Scrying is easier to work with at night-time under the light of the moon, but it can be done in the dark with a well-positioned candle. See what images appear on the surface of the water and try to decipher what they mean to you.

Ink Scrying

Using a similar method as water scrying in a bowl. Once you have filled it with water you drip droplets of coloured ink onto the surface using an eyedropper or paintbrush. Read the images and symbols that you see.

Dowsing

The art of dowsing was traditionally a method of divining for sources of underground water, but it can have other uses. The tool used in dowsing is usually a wooden Y shaped stick often from the hazel tree (although copper rods or pendulums are sometimes used as well). The Y part of the stick is held one side in each hand and the long part of the Y points forward. Sometimes two bent sticks or wires are used, one held in each hand. The sticks move when they find water or ley lines or whatever it is you are seeking.

Tea Leaf Reading (this can also be done with coffee grounds)

Tea leaf reading or tasseography is fairly simple to do, first of all you need to make a cup of tea…that was pretty obvious, wasn't it? You will need to use loose leaf tea made in a pot, let it steep for a few minutes (if you don't have loose leaf tea you can open up a tea bag). Whilst the tea is brewing use this time to ground and centre yourself and allow your mind to become calm. Then pour yourself a cup of tea, a plain light colour cup is best.

Slowly sip the tea (avoiding the tea leaves). If you have a question in mind, then think about it as you drink your tea. Leave a small amount of tea in your cup, then hold your nearly empty cup in your hand and swirl it around three times. The tea leaves should disperse around the inside of the cup. Carefully dump out the remaining liquid by turning your cup over into a saucer...wait for a count of three then turn your cup back over.

If your cup has a handle begin reading the tea leaves from that point working clockwise, if it has no handle start at the 12 o'clock position. Read what you see...

Puddle Scrying

Puddles can be found anywhere that it has rained it could be a muddy puddle in the middle of the woods or an oily puddle in the centre of the city either way they provide very good mirrors to scry with. Take a moment to ground and centre yourself then unfocus your eyes and gaze across the puddle. If you have a question, you can ask it, otherwise just ask what wisdom the water has for you. See what images you can find on the surface of the water. This works really well if the puddle has leaves or an oily surface as it provides a bit of movement.

Mirror Scrying

Mirrors obviously have a super reflective surface so they can be used for scrying just as you would scrying with the surface of water. You can use a regular mirror for this, ask your question, unfocus your eyes and look across the surface of the mirror and see what images you sense. A classic scrying mirror is a black one created from a dark concave surface, originally made from polished obsidian. You can make your own black mirror by taking an empty picture frame and painting the back of the glass with black paint.

Working with your mirror – keep the surface clean, charge, recharge and bless your mirror regularly, working on a full moon seems to work best for mirror magic, burn incense to heighten your psychic awareness whilst you work, work in the dark with candles and don't focus too hard on the mirrors surface, it is your mind's eye that should be doing the 'seeing'.

Exercise

Work with some of the water divination methods. See which one works best for you and what sort of results you get.

Astrology

For those of you that work with horoscopes, sun signs and moon signs. The twelve signs of the zodiac are split into the four elements. What we generally think of as our zodiac sign is the sun sign, we were born under. We usually take on a lot of the characteristics that the sign corresponds with, although we will also be affected by the moon sign we were born under as well. And of course, if you are working magic you can take into account the sign that the sun or moon is in to help boost your magic, which is what I am looking at here...

The water signs are:

Cancer – 21st June to 22nd July – sign of cardinal water.
Ruled by the Moon, emotional, sympathetic and a lover of the home but can be vulnerable and highly strung.
Qualities: Introspective, intuitive, likes security, emotional, determined, goals, enterprising, ambitious, shrewd, insightful, home, family, domestic peace, loyal, affectionate, kind, supportive, nurturing.

Symbol: The claws of the crab but also breasts of the mother.

Scorpio – 23rd October to 21st November – sign of fixed water. Ruled by Pluto, intense, magnetic and able to delve deep into psychological and intellectual areas. But can be obsessive, jealous and arrogant.

Qualities: Magnetic, passionate, vibrant, complex, perceptive, sensual, psychic abilities, observant, insightful, emotional, private, curious, mysteries, determination, focused, resourceful.

Symbol: The scorpion's tail or male genitals.

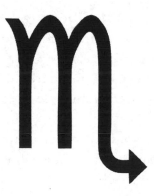

Pisces – 19th February to 19th March – sign of mutable water. Ruled by Neptune, compassionate, impressionable, gentle and imaginative but can be gullible and a wishful thinker.

Qualities: Sensitive, emotional, sympathetic, receptive, psychic, generous, insightful, spiritual, inspiring, intuitive, risk taking.

Symbol: Two fish tied together.

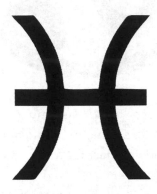

Exercise

Create some magical workings using the energy of the water zodiac signs. Try using them on the corresponding date. What were your results and experiences?

Water Blessing

Water has its own immense power, think about the destruction an ocean or deep fast flowing river can cause. Never underestimate its power. Water is cleansing and purifying, it is such a simple and easy element to work with to add to your magical practice.

Make offerings to your local water sources, but please keep them biodegradable and items that won't taint the water source (pebbles or shells are good).

Send blessings to the sky when it rains, for feeding the earth and nourishing the plants.

Give your thanks to the element of water each time you shower, wash your hands or take a bath, that we are able to have flowing water so easily available.

Water is indeed a magical element. Spend some time with your water source, sit beside it, paddle in it (if safe to do so) and connect with the energy.

Reference Books and Recommended Further Reading

A Kitchen Witch's World of Magical Herbs and Plants (Rachel Patterson)

Witchcraft into the Wild (Rachel Patterson)

A Kitchen Witch's World of Magical Food (Rachel Patterson)

Kitchen Witchcraft: Crystal Magic (Rachel Patterson)

Pagan Portals Animal Magic (Rachel Patterson)

Grimoire of a Kitchen Witch (Rachel Patterson)

The Witch's Cauldron (Laura Tempest Zakroff)

The Way of the Water Priestess (Annwyn Avalon)

Water Witchcraft (Annwyn Avalon)

The Sea Priestess (Dion Fortune)

www.theoi.com

www.britannica.com

www.ancient-symbols.com/

www.glendonbandb.co.uk/well-dressings-in-derbyshire/

www.cpre.org.uk/discover/well-dressing-an-ancient-art/

You may also enjoy

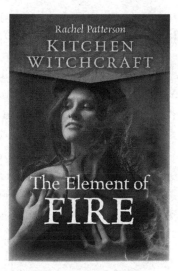

Kitchen Witchcraft: The Element of Fire
Rachel Patterson

The fifth in a series of books that delve into the world of the Kitchen Witch. Elements, rituals, spells, correspondences, meditations and practical suggestions

978-1-78904-721-9 (Paperback)
978-1-78904-722-6 (e-book)

MOON BOOKS
PAGANISM & SHAMANISM

What is Paganism? A religion, a spirituality, an alternative belief system, nature worship? You can find support for all these definitions (and many more) in dictionaries, encyclopaedias, and text books of religion, but subscribe to any one and the truth will evade you. Above all Paganism is a creative pursuit, an encounter with reality, an exploration of meaning and an expression of the soul. Druids, Heathens, Wiccans and others, all contribute their insights and literary riches to the Pagan tradition. Moon Books invites you to begin or to deepen your own encounter, right here, right now.

If you have enjoyed this book, why not tell other readers by posting a review on your preferred book site.

Bestsellers from Moon Books

Keeping Her Keys
An Introduction to Hekate's Modern Witchcraft
Cyndi Brannen
*Blending Hekate, witchcraft and personal development together
to create a powerful new magickal perspective.*
Paperback: 978-1-78904-075-3 ebook 978-1-78904-076-0

Journey to the Dark Goddess
How to Return to Your Soul
Jane Meredith
*Discover the powerful secrets of the Dark Goddess and transform
your depression, grief and pain into healing and integration.*
Paperback: 978-1-84694-677-6 ebook: 978-1-78099-223-5

Shamanic Reiki
Expanded Ways of Working with Universal Life Force Energy
Llyn Roberts, Robert Levy
*Shamanism and Reiki are each powerful ways of healing; together,
their power multiplies. Shamanic Reiki introduces techniques to
help healers and Reiki practitioners tap ancient healing wisdom.*
Paperback: 978-1-84694-037-8 ebook: 978-1-84694-650-9

Southern Cunning
Folkloric Witchcraft in the American South
Aaron Oberon
*Modern witchcraft with a Southern flair, this book is a journey
through the folklore of the American South and a look at the power
these stories hold for modern witches.*
Paperback: 978-1-78904-196-5 ebook: 978-1-78904-197-2

Readers of ebooks can buy or view any of these bestsellers by clicking on the live link in the title. Most titles are published in paperback and as an ebook. Paperbacks are available in traditional bookshops. Both print and ebook formats are available online.

Find more titles and sign up to our readers' newsletter
http://www.johnhuntpublishing.com/paganism

Follow us on Facebook
https://www.facebook.com/MoonBooks

Follow us on Instagram
https://www.instagram.com/moonbooksjhp/

Follow us on Twitter
https://twitter.com/MoonBooksJHP

Follow us on TikTok
https://www.tiktok.com/@moonbooksjhp